Summer Bridge Reading
Grades 2–3

Editor: Heather Canup, Julie Kirsch
Layout Design: Tiara Reynolds
Inside Illustrations: Magen Mitchell
Cover Design: Chasity Rice
Cover Illustration: Wayne Miller

ISBN 978-1-60022-445-4

Table of Contents

The *Summer Bridge Reading* series is designed to help children improve their reading skills during the summer months and between grades. *Summer Bridge Reading* includes several extra components to help make your child's study of reading easier and more inviting.

For example, an **Assessment** test has been included to help you determine your child's reading knowledge and what skills need improvement. Use this test, as well as the **Assessment Analysis**, as a diagnostic tool for those areas in which your child may need extra practice.

Furthermore, the **Incentive Contract** will motivate your child to complete the work in *Summer Bridge Reading*. Together, you and your child choose the reward for completing specific sections of the book. Check off the pages that your child has completed, and he or she will have a record of his or her accomplishment.

Examples are included for each new skill that your child will learn. The examples are located in blue boxes at the tops of the pages. On each page, the directions refer to the example your child needs to complete a specific type of activity.

Summer Reading List

Aliki
Ah, Music!

Bemelmans, Ludwig
Madeline

Blocksma, Mary
Yoo Hoo, Moon!

Brunhoff, Jean de
The Story of Babar

Christian, Mary Blount
Penrod's Picture

DiCamillo, Kate
Because of Winn-Dixie

Estes, Eleanor
The Hundred Dresses

Falconer, Ian
Olivia

Fleischman, Sid
McBroom Tells the Truth

Gannett, Ruth Stiles
My Father's Dragon

Gelman, Rita Golden
More Spaghetti, I Say!

Giff, Patricia Reilly
Today Was a Terrible Day

Himmelman, John
The Super Camper Caper

Honeycutt, Natalie
The All New Jonah Twist

Leaf, Munro
The Story of Ferdinand

Munsch, Robert
Stephanie's Ponytail

Muth, Jon J.
The Three Questions

O'Brien, Robert C.
The Silver Crown

Parish, Peggy
Amelia Bedelia

Paterson, Katherine
The Smallest Cow in the World

Rathmann, Peggy
Officer Buckle and Gloria

Roop, Peter and Connie
Keep the Lights Burning, Abbie

Sachar, Louis
Sideways Stories from Wayside School

Scieszka, Jon
The Stinky Cheese Man

Seuss, Dr.
Great Day for Up

Sharmat, Marjorie Weinman
Nate the Great

Steig, William
Sylvester and the Magic Pebble

Thompson, Kay
Eloise

Turner, Ann
Dust for Dinner

Trenc, Milan
The Night at the Museum

White, E. B.
Charlotte's Web

Williams, Margery
The Velveteen Rabbit

Yolen, Jane
Sleeping Ugly

Incentive Contract

List your agreed-upon incentive for each section below. Place an *X* after each completed exercise.

	Activity Title	X	My Incentive Is:
9	The Great Word Race		
10	The Same Meaning		
11	The Synonym Song		
13	Opposite Meanings		
14	Hot Air Antonyms		
15	Aunt Antonyms		
17	Many Meanings		
18	More Than One Meaning		
19	The Runt		
21	The Dead Sea		
23	Crustaceans		
24	Bird Nests		
25	Stamps		
26	It's All in the Details		
27	Birds		

	Activity Title	X	My Incentive Is:
29	Good Guess		
30	A Sunny Flower		
31	Cora and Corinne		
33	Sara and Katie		
34	Alike or Different?		
35	The Ostrich		
37	The Story of Soap		
38	Animal World		
39	Key Words		
40	The Midnight Ride		
41	Air Paths		
42	Bicycle Safety		
44	U.S. Presidents		
45	Which Word Does Not Belong?		
46	Animal Poem		
48	In a Neighborly Way		

	Activity Title	X	My Incentive Is:
49	Dear Donna		
51	Finding the Cause		
52	Stray Cat Hero		
54	A New Zealand Treat		
56	American Indian Dance		
57	Sea Horses		
59	Eight Minutes Over France		
61	What Happens?		
62	Miss Nelson		
63	Mammals or Birds?		
64	Who's Prince Charming?		
66	The Snow Child		
68	Ellen's Helpers		
69	The Musicians of Bremen		
70	The Ants Go Marching		

	Activity Title	X	My Incentive Is:
72	What Happened?		
73	Dialogue Detectives		
74	The Money Plant		
77	Entry Words		
78	Using Guide Words		
79	Finding Words		
80	Mistaken Identity		
82	Animals		
83	The Library		
85	What's In Here?		
86	Betsy Ross		
88	Look It Up		
89	Driver Ants		
91	Assignments		
92	Television Schedule		

Assessment Test

1. Circle the word that means the same as the underlined word.

   The swift rabbit escaped from the chasing fox.

   A. slow **B.** baby
   C. quick **D.** furry

2. Circle the word that means the opposite of the underlined word.

   Mom gave me an extra dollar in my allowance because my room looked immaculate.

   A. clean **B.** tidy
   C. messy **D.** funny

3. In which sentence does the underlined word have the same meaning as the underlined word in the sentence below?

   My teacher asked us to take out a sheet of paper.

   A. The roads have become a sheet of ice.
   B. The nurse wrapped a sheet around the sleeping baby.
   C. Have you seen my sheet of homework assignments?
   D. We used an old sheet as the roof for our fort.

4. Which sentence is a fact?

   A. Saturn is the coolest planet because it has rings.
   B. Life does not exist on Earth.
   C. Jupiter is the largest planet.
   D. Mars is the most interesting planet because of its color.

5. Circle the letter of the word that does not belong.

   A. pig **B.** horse
   C. barn **D.** sheep

6. What is found at the end of informational books?

   A. Title page **B.** Index
   C. Table of contents **D.** Dictionary entry

Assessment Test

7. Which conclusion best fits the sentence below?

Brenda grabbed a bagel from the refrigerator, threw her backpack over her shoulder, and ran for the bus.

A. She is late for school.
B. She is mad at someone.
C. She already ate.
D. She has to feed the dog.

8. Your teacher asks you to write a poem about your birthday party. What might you name it?

A. Pizza Party
B. Decorating with Balloons
C. Best Friends
D. My Surprise Party

9. Which of these happens first?

A. Soon, I will walk to the library.
B. Eventually, I will go to the store.
C. First, I need to go to school.
D. Someday, I will go to the football game.

10. Using the information given, which sentence is not a logical inference?

When Westin got home, he found that the bird's nest was empty.

A. The eggs hatched, and the birds flew away.
B. The eggs were stolen by a nest-robbing dinosaur.
C. The eggs were eaten by a snake.
D. The eggs were blown out of the nest in a thunderstorm.

11. Write two similarities and two differences between yourself and a family member.

Similarities:

1. ____________________

2. ____________________

Differences:

1. ____________________

2. ____________________

Assessment Test

Read each passage and answer the questions.

Jason heard the garbage truck coming and remembered that his job wasn't done yet.

12. What was Jason's job?

A. to deliver newspapers
B. to walk the dog
C. to water the plants
D. to take out the trash

13. What will probably happen next in the story?

A. Jason ran toward the garage and quickly wheeled the trash cans outside.
B. Jason waved to the garbage truck driver.
C. Jason went back to reading his book.
D. Jason went downstairs to finish the dishes.

Jenny threw herself on her bed and buried her head in a pillow.

14. How do you think Jenny is feeling?

A. proud
B. sad
C. cheerful
D. clever

The cat jumped into Mom's lap and she spilled her coffee.

15. What was the cause of Mom spilling her coffee?

A. Mom is clumsy.
B. The cat tripped Mom.
C. The cat jumped into Mom's lap.
D. Mom was mad at the cat.

My sister always forgets things. Last week, she left her math book at our grandmother's house. Yesterday, she left her lunch at home. Today, she left her field trip money. Who knows what she will forget tomorrow?

16. Where did the sister leave her math book?

A. home
B. school
C. her friend's house
D. her grandmother's house

Assessment Analysis

Answer Key:

1. C.
2. C.
3. C.
4. C.
5. C.
6. B.
7. A.
8. D.
9. C.
10. B.
11. Answers will vary.
12. D.
13. A.
14. B.
15. C.
16. D.

After reviewing your student's assessment test, match the problems answered incorrectly to the corresponding activity pages. Spend extra time on those skills to ensure that your student strengthens his reading skills.

Problem	Skill	Activity Pages
1.	synonyms	9–12
2.	antonyms	13–16
3.	homonyms	17–20
4.	fact or opinion	56–58
5.	classification	44–47
6.	drawing conclusions	59–65
7.	main idea	21–23
8.	parts of a book	82–87
9.	sequencing	37–40
10.	making inferences	70–76
11.	compare and contrast	33–36
12.	drawing conclusions	59–65
13.	predicting outcomes	66–69
14.	character analysis	48–50
15.	cause and effect	51–55
16.	reading for details	24–28

The Great Word Race

synonyms

Synonyms are words that have almost the same meaning.
Example: complete, finish

Find a synonym on the racetrack for each word below. Write the number of each word from the list next to the matching word on the racetrack. Be sure to work in order to move the race cars forward. Circle the car that wins the Great Word Race!

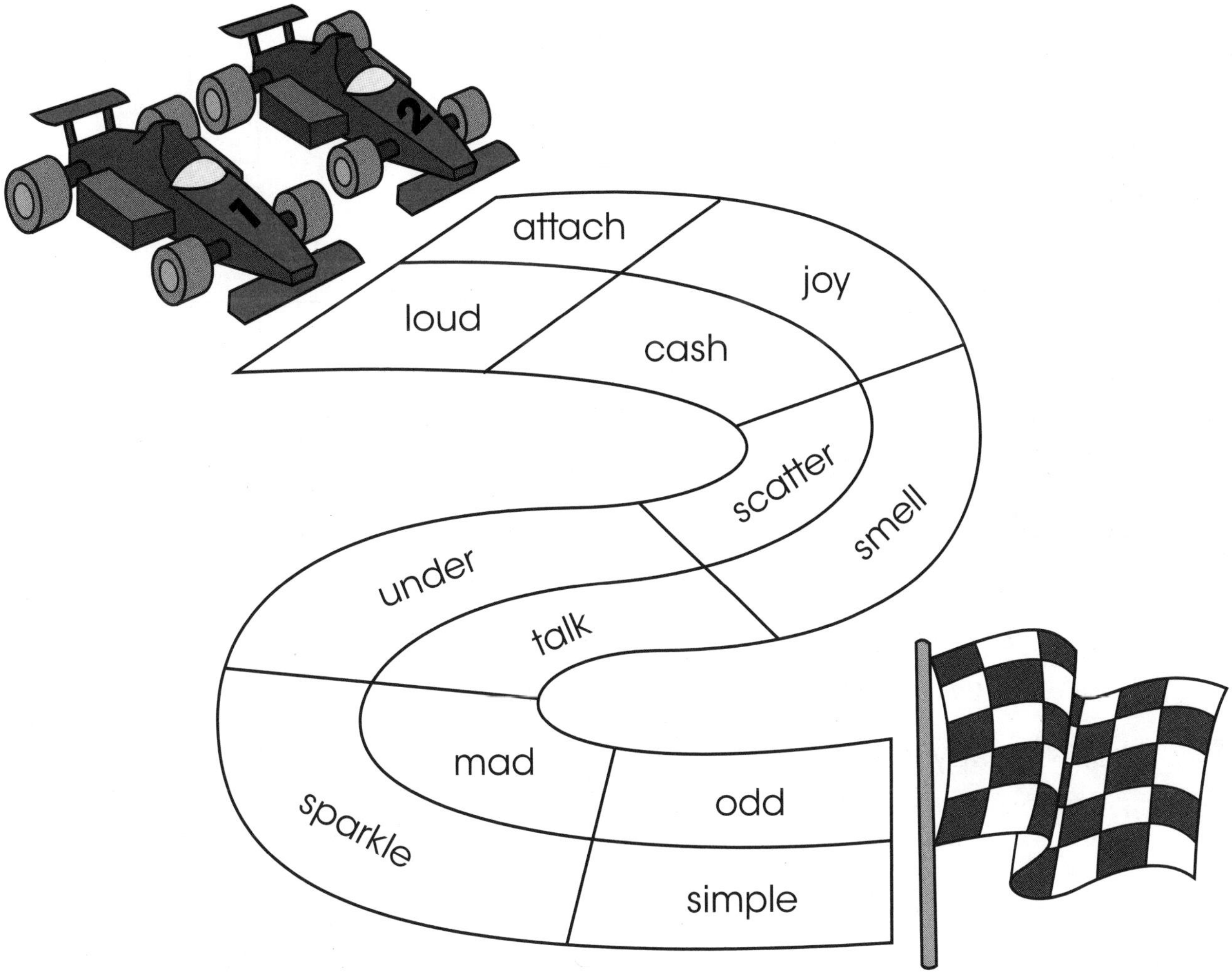

attach
loud
joy
cash
scatter
smell
under
talk
mad
odd
sparkle
simple

1.	connect	**2.**	noisy	**3.**	money	**4.**	happiness
5.	spread	**6.**	beneath	**7.**	scent	**8.**	speak
9.	angry	**10.**	glitter	**11.**	strange		

The Same Meaning

synonyms

Complete the puzzle by finding the synonym of the bold word. Use the words in the word bank.

remember	smart	doctor	great
grabbed	starving	crowd	bite

Down

1. My mom took me to our **physician** when I got sick.
2. My dog is so **intelligent** that he learned three new tricks in one day.
3. There was a huge **mob** of fans outside the concert.
4. My aunt **grasped** the railing as she came down the stairs.
5. Jack's puppy likes to **gnaw** on his bone.

Across

6. Do you **recall** the phone number?
7. I ate two plates of spaghetti because I was **famished**.
8. Your birthday party was **superb**!

The Synonym Song

The words *small*, *tiny*, and *little* are **synonyms**. They are different words that mean the same thing. This song is full of synonyms.

Read the song below.

Sometimes I talk, but other times I...

shout, whisper, yell, discuss, chatter, or gab.

Sometimes I walk, but other times I...

saunter, tromp, march, step, stroll, trudge, or trek.

Sometimes I run, but other times I...

skip, dash, flee, race, scramble, or scurry.

Sometimes I jump, but other times I...

leap, hop, spring, bound, or vault.

Sometimes I laugh, but other times I...

giggle, chuckle, titter, cackle, or snicker.

Sometimes I sleep, but other times I...

slumber, rest, doze, nap, or snooze.

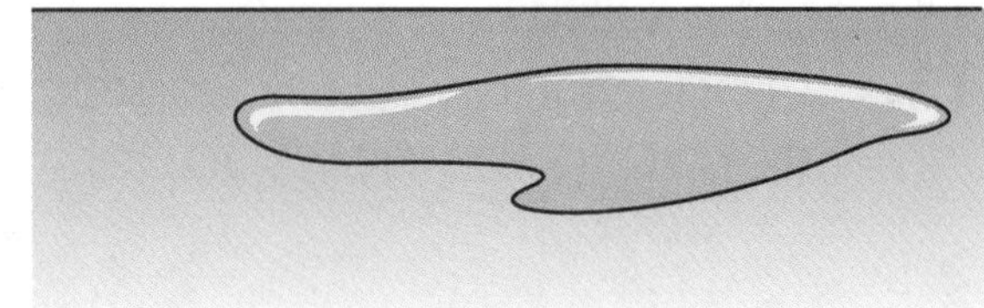

The Synonym Song

1. What is a synonym?
   - **A.** a word that means the opposite of another word
   - **B.** a word that sounds like another word but has a different meaning
   - **C.** a word that means the same as another word

Draw a line between the synonyms.

2.	talk	leap
3.	walk	snooze
4.	run	giggle
5.	jump	chatter
6.	laugh	stroll
7.	sleep	dash

Circle the word in parentheses that would fit best in each sentence.

8. I will (whisper / shout) a secret in your ear.
9. I will (saunter / march) to the rhythm of the drum.
10. I will (skip / dash) to get some help.
11. I will (cry / laugh) during the funny movie.
12. I will (slumber / nap) all night.
13. I (chuckled / cackled) at the comic in the newspaper.

A **thesaurus** is a book that lists synonyms of words. You can use a thesaurus to make your writing more interesting. Look at this page from a thesaurus. Then, answer the questions below.

> **sad (adj)**: unhappy, down, dismal, morose, miserable, cheerless, gloomy, forlorn, dejected, glum, depressed
>
> **said (v)**: spoke, yelled, whispered, echoed, bellowed, whined, shouted, told, mentioned

14. What does the (adj) after the word *sad* tell you? ____________

    ____

15. Rewrite this sentence using a synonym for the word *sad*.
    The boy was feeling sad because he lost his puppy.

    ____

    ____

    ____

16. Write at least three synonyms for the word *big*.

    ____

    ____

    ____

Opposite Meanings

antonyms

Antonyms are words with opposite meanings.
Example: raise, lower

Read each word below. Then, find its antonym in the word bank and write it in the boxes. To find the answer to the riddle, read the letters in the bold boxes.

adult	brave	remember	silent	cheap	filthy
whole	begin	dangerous	stretch	playful	catch

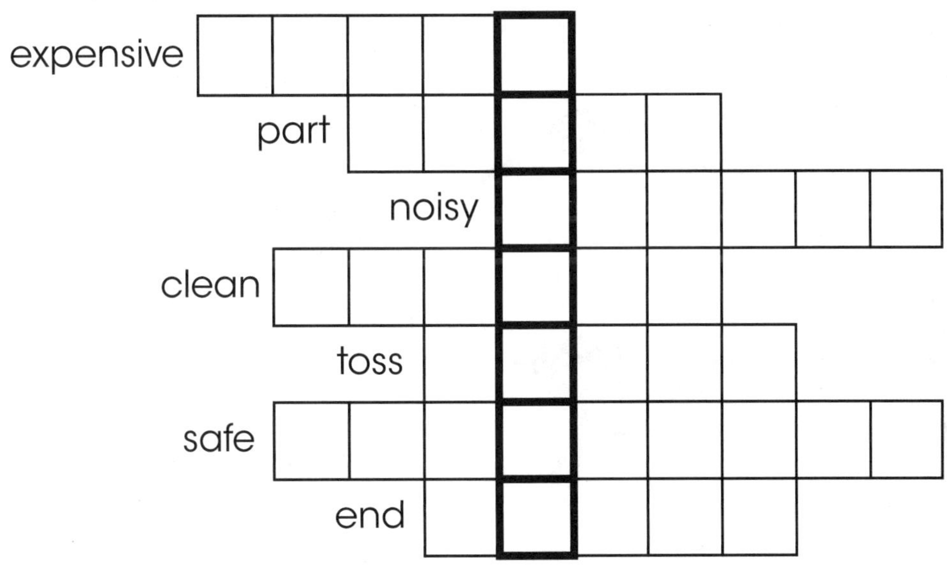

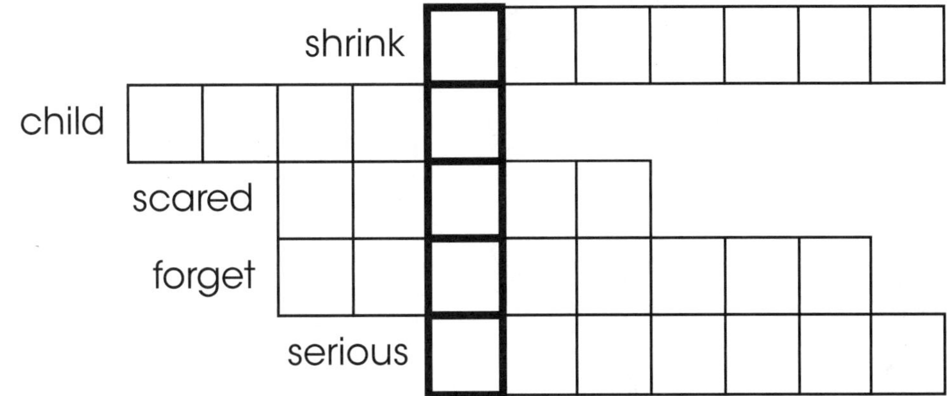

What travels all around the world, yet always stays in the corner?

A ___ ___ ___ ___ ___ ___ ___ ___ ___ ___ ___ ___!

Hot Air Antonyms

Find the antonym in the word bank for each bold word. Write the letter for each antonym on the matching balloon basket.

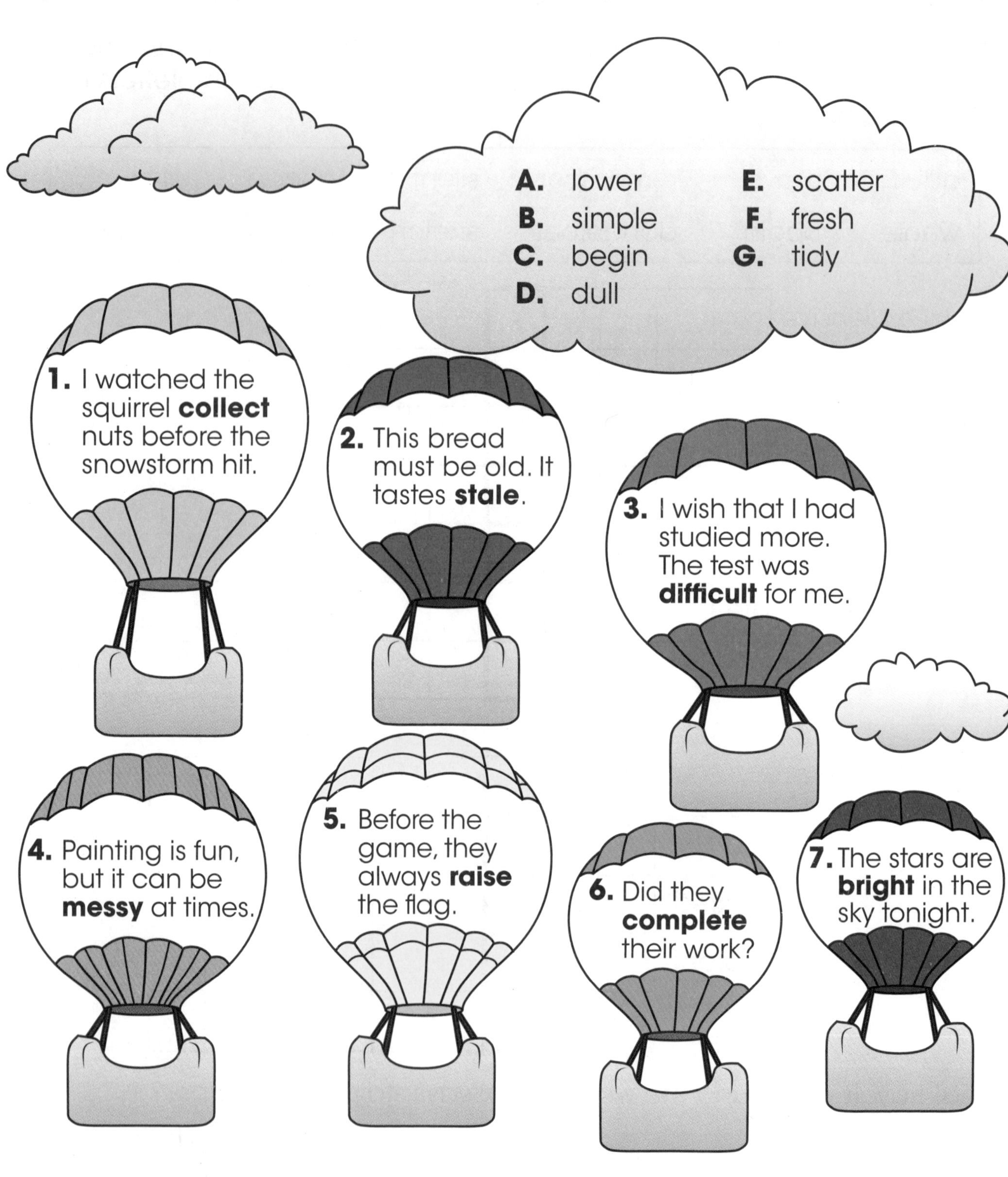

Aunt Antonym

antonyms

Read the story below.

We have a nickname for my mother's sister. We call her Aunt Antonym. She always says or does the opposite of what we say or do. At the zoo, we began at the north end of the park. My aunt began at the south end. At the monkey cage, we thought the monkeys were adorable. My aunt thought they were ugly. I said a zebra is a white horse with black stripes. My aunt said a zebra is a black horse with white stripes. At the dolphin show, we sat in the front. We like getting wet. My aunt sat in the back. She wanted to stay dry. Soon, we were hungry. My aunt was still full from breakfast. After lunch, we rode the train around the zoo. My aunt wanted to walk. Finally, my aunt said she was ready to go. We wished we could have stayed.

Aunt Antonym

Write *T* before the statements that are true and *F* before the statements that are false.

____ **1.** The author is writing about his sister.

____ **2.** Aunt Antonym is the real name of the author's aunt.

____ **3.** Aunt Antonym thinks monkeys are ugly.

____ **4.** Aunt Antonym wanted to sit in the back at the dolphin show because she didn't like to get wet.

Answer in a complete sentence.

5. Why did the author call his aunt Aunt Antonym?

____

____

____

____

An **antonym** is a word that means the opposite of another word. For example, an antonym of *big* is *little*. Write a word from the story that is an antonym for each word below.

6. north ____________

7. ugly ____________

8. black ____________

9. front ____________

10. dry ____________

11. hungry ____________

Write the past tense for each verb.

12. begin ____________

13. think ____________

14. say ____________

15. ride ____________

16. sit ____________

Many Meanings

Some words have more than one meaning. These words are called **homonyms**. You can tell which meaning is being used from the context clues of the sentence.

Write the homonym from the word bank that makes sense with the context clues in each pair of sentences.

tire	break	mean	straw	land	glasses	book	free

1. Be careful not to ________________ Mom's favorite vase.
   Should we take a ________________ from practice to eat lunch?

2. Mom will ________________ an appointment for Monday.
   Have you read the new ________________ by that author?

3. What do you ________________ by that?
   The dog that lives next door is ________________, so let's stay away.

4. My cat is so old that chasing a mouse will ________________ her out.
   We got a flat ________________ when we drove to Florida.

5. The plane is due to ________________ at 6:00 tonight.
   The large areas of ________________ on Earth are called continents.

6. The zookeeper lifted the door to ________________ the bird.
   I can't believe we read enough books to earn ________________ pizza!

7. After you finish, set your lemonade ________________ on the counter.
   I am going to get new ________________ to help me see the board.

8. The farmer keeps ________________ in the barn during the winter.
   Can you hand me a ________________ for my milk shake?

More Than One Meaning

A **dictionary** will help you discover the multiple meanings of a word.

The words below are homonyms. Write two sentences that use different meanings for each word.

park

1. ______________________________

____

2. ______________________________

____

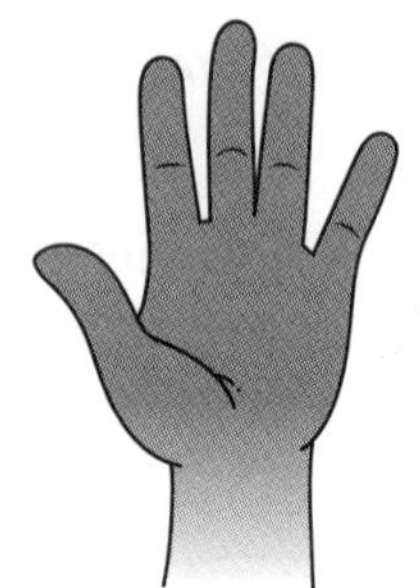

hand

3. ______________________________

____

4. ______________________________

____

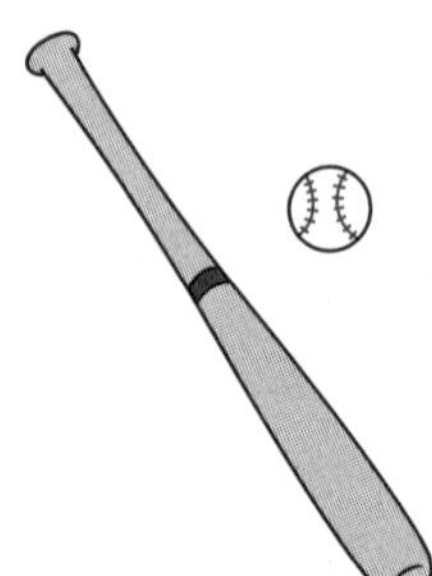

bat

5. ______________________________

____

6. ______________________________

____

The Runt

Every spring, my dad lets me choose one of the piglets from the litter to raise. I raise the piglet to show at the county fair. Pigs that show well at the fair sell for a good price. Dad lets me keep the money I earn from the pig, so I work hard each year to raise my pig.

This year, our sow had nine piglets. I usually choose the biggest and the strongest of the litter, but this year the runt caught my eye. The runt is the smallest pig of the litter. Usually, the runt is too small to get to the sow to feed it. But, this runt was a fighter. I sat in the pen watching the piglets step over each other. They were fighting to be first to the sow. The runt, however, came and nuzzled up to me. It was as if he thought that I had milk for him. I picked the runt up and took him to the house. Dad was surprised that I picked the runt of the litter. But, I told Dad that I would make this runt into a prize pig.

Through the spring and summer I fed the runt. He grew and grew. By fall, he was ready to eat slop and grain. I took good care of my little pig. By spring, the little runt had grown into the biggest pig I had ever seen. My little runt won first prize at the county fair. He wasn't so little anymore.

The Runt

1. What is the main idea of the story?
   A. raising a runt
   B. growing up on a farm
   C. going to the fair

2. Put a *T* if the sentence is true. Put an *F* if the sentence is false.

____ The runt always grows up to be the biggest pig of the litter.

____ The runt won first prize at the fair.

____ The writer of the story earns money from selling pigs.

____ The sow had nine piglets.

3. Draw a line between each word and its definition.

piglet	a group of baby pigs from one mother
sow	to help grow up
litter	cuddled
nuzzled	baby pig
raise	mother pig

4. What does *runt* mean in this story?
   A. a type of candy
   B. the smallest piglet in a litter
   C. the biggest piglet in a litter

5. What does the idiom *caught my eye* mean?
   A. got something in my eye
   B. scared me
   C. got my attention

Many words have more than one meaning. The different meanings are numbered in the dictionary. Read each word and its meanings. Write the number of the correct meaning before each sentence.

raise	1. To care for a baby until it is an adult. 2. To lift something up.

____ **6.** Mrs. Crosby said to raise your hand.

____ **7.** I am going to raise my puppy, Sinbad.

pen	1. An instrument used to write. 2. A fenced area where an animal is kept.

____ **8.** Marley took my green pen to do her homework.

____ **9.** There are six piglets in the pen.

slop	1. Food given to animals. 2. When liquid spills over sides of a container.

____ **10.** Teresa tried to be careful, but I saw the soup slop out of the bowl.

____ **11.** Lexi gathered up the food scraps for the pigs' slop.

The Dead Sea

The main idea of a passage tells what the passage is about. It does not tell one part or fact from the passage. It is an overview of the entire passage or paragraph. Titles often tell you something about the main idea.

Which title best describes the passage below?

Tall Buildings in the U.S. *The Sears Tower*

The Sears Tower is the world's tallest building. It is even taller than the Empire State Building in New York City. The Sears Tower has 110 stories and is 1,707 feet tall (including its antenna towers on top). When the sky is clear, visitors on top of the building can see into four states!

The best title is *The Sears Tower* because the whole passage is about the Sears Tower. The Empire State Building is mentioned, but only to compare it with the Sears Tower.

Each title below describes the main idea for a different passage on page 22. Write each title at the top of its matching passage. Remember to ask yourself, "Does this title tell about the whole passage?"

The Water Cycle of the Dead Sea
What Is the Dead Sea?
The Uses of the Dead Sea
The Salty Waters of the Dead Sea

The Dead Sea

main idea

Use the titles on page 21 to tell the main idea of each passage below.

____________________ ____________________	____________________ ____________________
1. The Dead Sea is a saltwater lake in Asia, located between Jordan and Israel. The northern part of the lake is the deepest, measuring about 2,622 feet below sea level. At the southern end of the Dead Sea, a shallow area is partly cut off by a peninsula.	**2.** The Dead Sea is nearly nine times saltier than the ocean! The salt is so thick that very little plant or animal life can survive in its waters. The sea is believed to have gotten its name for this reason. If a person tries to swim in the Dead Sea, he will float on top!
____________________ ____________________	____________________ ____________________
3. The Dead Sea is useful for many reasons. Its salt is mined easily and inexpensively. Its waters are used for beauty and health reasons. Many queens, kings, and famous people have been to the sea for health or beauty reasons. Thousands of people still visit the sea in hopes of curing skin and bone problems.	**4.** The Dead Sea gets water from a river to the north called the Jordan River, which empties into the sea. Other smaller streams also feed water into the Dead Sea, mostly from the east. There are no rivers that lead out of the sea, so the water stays there until it evaporates. Because the Dead Sea is located in the desert, evaporation is fast!

Crustaceans

Longer passages may be written in paragraphs. Each paragraph should tell about something different. In this case, the title should be about the entire passage. Each paragraph will have a topic sentence that tells about that paragraph's main idea.

Choose a title to describe the main idea of the entire passage below. Then, choose the topic sentence for each paragraph. Circle your answers.

Lobsters are saltwater animals that belong to a group called *crustaceans*. They have a hard outer shell and five sets of legs. The first set of legs has claws. One claw is usually used for crushing, and the other for biting. The female lobster lays thousands of eggs. The tiny young drift and swim for three to five weeks before settling on the bottom of the ocean.

Crayfish are freshwater cousins of lobsters. Crawfish, as they are also called, may be as short as two inches in length. Like their lobster cousins, crayfish have large front claws that are actually one of five sets of legs. Crayfish are found around the world in freshwater rivers and streams, except in Africa and Antarctica.

1. A good title for this passage would be:
- **A.** River Animals
- **B.** Lobsters
- **C.** Cousins with Claws

2. The topic sentence in the first paragraph is:
- **A.** The first set of legs has claws.
- **B.** They have a hard outer shell and five sets of legs.
- **C.** Lobsters are saltwater animals that belong to a group called *crustaceans*.

3. The topic sentence in the second paragraph is:
- **A.** Crawfish, as they are also called, may be as short as two inches in length.
- **B.** Crayfish are freshwater cousins of lobsters.
- **C.** Crayfish are found in freshwater rivers and streams.

Bird Nests

reading for details

Read the passage below. Then, answer the questions.

Birds make nests in many places. Woodpeckers make nests in tree trunks. Crows build them in high branches. A quail digs a shallow hole under a bush for a nest. Some desert owls build nests inside cacti. Swallows build mud nests under bridges. Wherever they live, birds find safe places to raise their babies.

1. Name four places birds can make nests.

____________________ ____________________

____________________ ____________________

2. Why do birds make nests?

____

3. Where do woodpeckers build their nests?

____

4. What kind of bird builds mud nests under bridges?

____

5. What kind of bird builds a nest in a cactus?

____

Extra!

Pretend you are a bird. Write a story about building your nest. How do you choose the best spot? What do you use to make your nest soft and warm? What problems do you have? Draw a picture to go with your story.

Stamps

Read the passage below. Then, answer the questions.

Some people save stamps. They keep their stamps in albums. They like to look at them. Some people like stamps that are very old. Some people like pretty stamps. Some people like stamps from places that are far away. Some stamps are worth a lot of money. Stamps that were printed incorrectly can be worth the most.

1. Where do some people keep their stamps?

____

2. Why do they keep them?

____

3. Name two kinds of stamps that people keep.

____

4. What kinds of stamps can be worth the most?

____

Extra!

Draw a stamp of your own on an envelope. Could you mail a letter with your stamp? Why or why not?

It's All in the Details

Supporting details are the parts of a paragraph that tell more about the topic sentence. They describe the main idea in more detail. The bold phrases below are supporting details.

Jeffrey was having a great day until his mom told him that he had to share his pet snake with his sister. He knew that **Lana would scream and scare his new best friend**. Besides, Lana had been playing dress-up, and **she smelled like a perfume bottle**. **No pet snake should have to smell like that**.

In each paragraph below, circle the topic sentence and underline two supporting details.

1. Some people like the fire department at the end of our street, and some people do not. My mom and dad think it is great because help could reach us within minutes. Nan's parents do not like it because of all the noise the sirens make. I guess I can see both sides.

2. Every evening, Gabriel and his dad look forward to feeding the deer in their backyard. Gabriel carries the dried corn from the garage to the edge of the woods. He and his dad spread the corn, then hide behind the edge of the house to watch. Each evening, the same four deer come to feed. Maybe someday they will have a newcomer!

3. Allie worked hard to finish all of her projects at summer camp. She tie-dyed her shirt in shades of blue and purple. She glued eyes onto her lion mask. Allie also carefully formed a monkey out of clay. Now, it was time for her favorite camp "project," lunch!

Birds

Read the passage below.

Birds are unique animals. Birds have wings, feathers, and beaks. Birds are the only animals that have feathers. Feathers enable most birds to fly. Their ability to fly helps them stay alive because they can hunt for food, escape their enemies, and migrate away from bad weather. Feathers also protect birds from getting too hot or too cold. Birds have beaks, but they do not have teeth. They use their beaks to get food. Birds eat insects, worms, seeds, and grains.

Birds are protective parents. They lay eggs and build nests to protect their eggs. Usually, the mother bird sits on the nest to keep the eggs warm. Both the mother and father bird keep watch over the nest before the eggs hatch. Nests continue to keep baby birds warm after they hatch from their eggs. Adult birds take care of baby birds until they are ready to fly. They bring food to the baby birds in the nest.

Birds

1. Circle the sentence that tells the main idea.
   - **A.** Birds are unique animals.
   - **B.** The adult bird teaches its babies how to fly and find food.
   - **C.** Birds are one of the few animals that lay eggs.

Fill in the blanks with the correct answers.

2. Birds are the only animals that have ________________.
3. Birds do not have __________.
4. Birds lay ________________.
5. Birds build ________________ to protect their eggs.
6. Number the sentences in the order that they happen.

____ The adult birds bring food to the baby birds in the nest.

____ The mother bird sits on the nest to keep the eggs warm.

____ Birds build a nest to protect their eggs.

____ The adult birds teach their babies how to fly and find food.

7. Write a *T* if the sentence is true. Write an *F* if the sentence is false.

____ All birds can fly.

____ Flying helps birds find food.

____ Flying protects birds from their enemies.

____ Birds migrate to stay away from their enemies.

____ Some birds have large teeth.

8. What does *migrate* mean?
   - **A.** to hide under trees
   - **B.** to fly to other places
   - **C.** to find shelter

Action verbs tell what the subject of a sentence does. Circle the action verb in each sentence.

9. Birds fly using their feathers.
10. Birds eat with their beaks instead of teeth.
11. Birds build nests to protect their eggs.
12. Baby birds hatch from eggs.
13. Adult birds bring their baby birds food.

Good Guess

Sometimes, context clues along with your own ideas will help you make a good guess at a word's meaning.

Use the context clues to make the best choice for each bold word's meaning.

1. Most small children are **forbidden** to cross the street without an adult.

A. helped **B.** told not to **C.** forced

2. Tracy buttoned her **cardigan** to keep warm at the game.

A. sweater **B.** pajamas **C.** boots

3. The autumn morning **dew** left the playground damp.

A. clumps of dirt **B.** pieces of ice **C.** drops of water

4. Dad likes to **relax** on the sofa after he takes us swimming.

A. jump **B.** rest **C.** eat

5. Our team must be **unified** if we want to win the championship.

A. work together **B.** awake **C.** dressed up

6. I remember that type of butterfly by its **distinct** markings.

A. yellow **B.** special **C.** dirty

7. The balloon **burst** as it brushed against the brick wall.

A. flew higher **B.** got away **C.** popped

8. Some American Indians made their **dwellings** in the caves.

A. shoes **B.** blankets **C.** homes

A Sunny Flower

Sometimes, the details you are looking for are words that you have never seen before. Remember to use the context of a sentence to help you learn about the new word.

The sunflower grows from a seed. First, a sunflower plant begins to grow a strong taproot. Soon, the green stalk begins to grow toward the warmth of the sun. As the plant grows, it forms a bud that will someday become a flower. The plant faces the east as the sun rises in the morning. Then, it follows the sun across the sky until it is facing west when the sun sets. As the flower's bud blooms, it unfolds into large, golden petals. The center of the flower is full of seeds. The seeds are either eaten or planted so that more sunflowers can grow.

Use details from the passage to complete the puzzle below. If you are unsure of a word's meaning, use context clues to help you.

Down

1. This passage is about the ______ .
4. The bud ______ into a flower
5. The ______ is like a stem.

Across

1. A sunflower grows toward the ______ .
2. Seeds grow in the ______ of the flower.
3. Sunflowers have large, golden ______ .
4. The plant forms a ______ that will become a flower.
6. The ______ begins to grow from the seed into the soil.

1. 2. 3. 4. 5. 6.

Cora and Corinne

Read the story below.

Corinne always loved visiting her grandma. Grandma Cora lived down the street on the next block. Her old stucco house was painted a dark, peachy pink.

"Coral, that's the color," her grandma would say. "I was named after the color coral because that's the color I was when I was born. You were going to be named after me, honey. You are my spittin' image. Besides, coral is the color of your hair. But, your daddy wanted you to have your own name, so your parents settled on Corinne. See how everything in life just ties up neat and tidy!"

Corinne always called her grandma "Cora." Cora once said, "I'm not old enough to be called 'Grandma.' Besides, I don't even feel like one."

Corinne and Cora were sitting in Cora's living room one crisp fall day. Corinne asked her grandma if she remembered going on the camping trip by the Potomac River in August. They had set up camp, then taken a boat trip. The boat ride had been long, and everyone was starving when it was over. When they got back to camp, they saw that Jonathan had forgotten to cover the food. Ants were all over it.

Jonathan cried because Corinne said she wished he hadn't come along. Everyone was so grumpy that they decided to pack and go home. Trying to make Jonathan feel better, Aunt Margy giggled and said she always liked ants. She was one, after all.

All of a sudden, it started to rain cats and dogs, and everything was getting wet. The dripping campers had to slog through the mud back to the car. By the time they got to Cora's jeep, sopping wet and muddy, they looked like something the cat had dragged in. Cora put in the key and turned it. Nothing happened. The battery was as dead as a doornail.

Cora and Corinne

A possessive pronoun takes the place of a possessive noun. Circle the correct pronoun for each sentence.

1. _____ hair is the color of coral.
   I **My**
2. We went to visit ___________ grandma down the street.
   she **her**
3. Everyone knew that it was _____ mistake.
   his **he**
4. The fire stopped _____ laughter.
   their **they**
5. Cora said to keep _____ eyes peeled.
   you **your**

An *idiom* is a phrase that means something different than what it seems to mean. Circle the letter of the best meaning for each phrase.

6. You are my spittin' image.
   - **A.** I have a picture of you spitting.
   - **B.** We look a lot alike.
   - **C.** We both like to spit.
7. They looked like something the cat dragged in.
   - **A.** A cat had attacked them.
   - **B.** They looked awful.
   - **C.** Their cat had come inside through the pet door.
8. It started to rain cats and dogs.
   - **A.** Cats and dogs were dropping from the sky.
   - **B.** It was raining hard.
   - **C.** The rain sounded like dogs barking.

Circle the letter of the best meaning for each bold word.

9. It was a crisp **fall** day.
   - **A.** autumn
   - **B.** to drop down to the ground
   - **C.** to be defeated
10. They **settled** on the best name for the baby.
    - **A.** paid a bill
    - **B.** sank
    - **C.** agreed

Sara and Katie

compare and contrast

Read each pair of sentences. If they tell how Sara's life is the same as Katie's, circle the word *same*. If they tell how Sara's life is different from Katie's, circle the word *different*.

A girl named Katie lives in a desert town not far from Sara's home. In some ways, Katie's life is like Sara's. In other ways, their lives are very different.

1.	Sara is a desert tortoise. Katie is a girl.	same	different
2.	Sara lives in a burrow. Katie lives in a house.	same	different
3.	Sara eats in the morning. Katie does, too.	same	different
4.	Sara can live for more than 60 years. Katie can, too.	same	different
5.	Sara does not have wings. Katie doesn't either.	same	different
6.	Sara can go for years without drinking water. Katie needs water every day.	same	different
7.	Sara sleeps all winter. Katie does not.	same	different
8.	Sara has four legs. Katie has two.	same	different

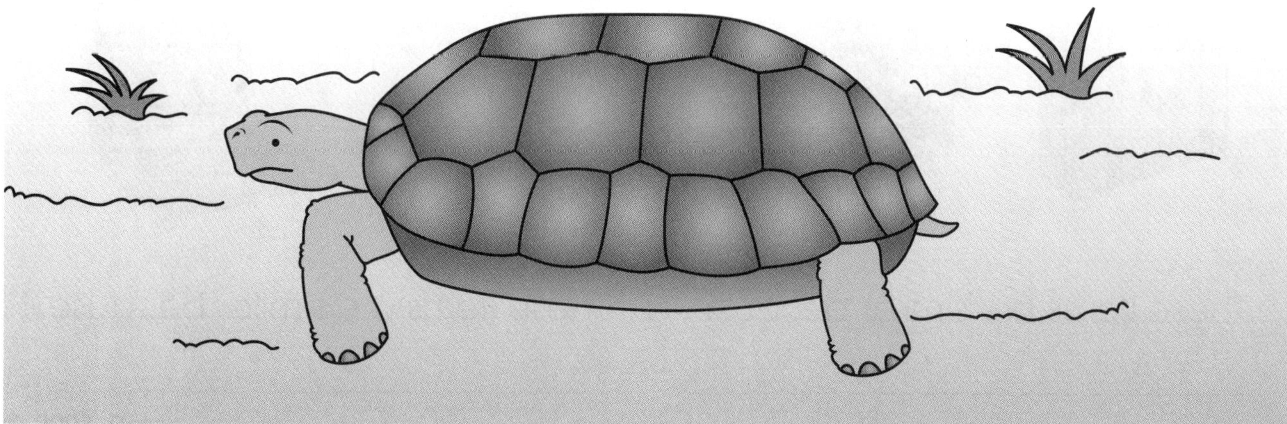

Extra!
Think of more ways Sara and Katie are the same.

Alike or Different?

compare and contrast

Part of reading carefully is watching for ways that things are alike (similarities) and ways that they are different (differences).

Each of the items below are probably familiar to you. Imagine that you are comparing them for a friend who cannot see them. How are the two items in each pair alike? How are they different? Write one similarity and one difference for each pair.

1.

These items are similar because

_______________________________ .

These items are different because

_______________________________ .

2.

These items are similar because

_______________________________ .

These items are different because

_______________________________ .

3.

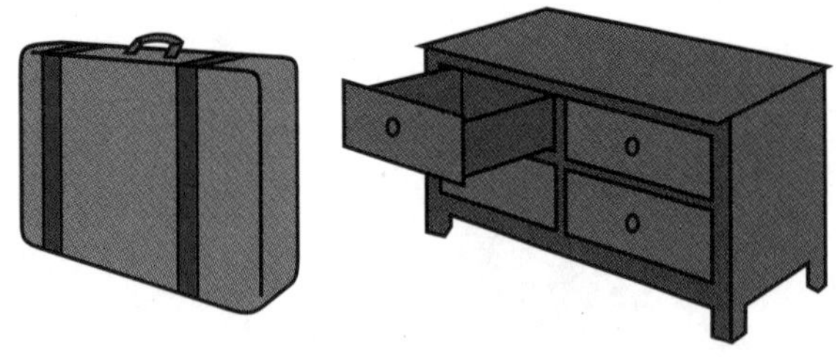

These items are similar because

_______________________________ .

These items are different because

_______________________________ .

4.

These items are similar because

_______________________________ .

These items are different because

_______________________________ .

The Ostrich

Read the passage below.

The ostrich is a unique bird. It is the largest bird. It can grow to be eight feet tall and can weigh more than 200 pounds. Unlike most other birds, the ostrich cannot fly. Its long legs help it run very fast. It runs with its wings outstretched. It uses its strong legs to protect itself, and the ostrich will run or kick if threatened.

The ostrich lays eggs and has feathers like other birds. Its eggs are extremely large. In fact, its eggs are almost the size of a football and can weigh nearly three pounds. The male ostrich digs a hole in the ground for a nest. The female ostrich lays her eggs in the hole. Then, both parents protect the eggs until the chicks hatch. Often, the female sits on the eggs during the day, and the male sits on the eggs during the night. After the chicks hatch, the parents continue to be very protective until the chicks can take care of themselves.

The Ostrich

1. Circle the letter of the sentence that tells the main idea.
   - **A.** The ostrich is the largest bird.
   - **B.** The ostrich is one of the most unique of all birds.
   - **C.** The ostrich lays eggs and has feathers like other birds.

2. Write a *T* if the sentence is true. Write an *F* if the sentence is false.

____ **A.** The ostrich can fly.

____ **B.** The ostrich can run very fast.

____ **C.** The mother ostrich lays its eggs in a hole in the ground.

____ **D.** The ostrich cannot kick without falling down.

3. Compare the ostrich to other birds. Put an *X* in the boxes to show whether each characteristic describes the ostrich, other birds, or both.

ostrich		other birds
☐	can fly	☐
☐	has/have feathers	☐
☐	lays eggs	☐
☐	grows to be 8 feet tall	☐
☐	protective of young	☐

Complete each sentence by circling the correct homophone.

4. The ostrich can grow to be ________ feet tall.

   ate eight

5. The ostrich can weigh more than ________ hundred pounds.

   too two

6. The ostrich egg can ________ nearly three pounds.

   way weigh

7. The ________ ostrich digs a hole in the ground for the nest.

   mail male

The ending *-er* sometimes means "more." It may be used to compare two things. The ending *-est* means "most." It is used to compare more than two things. If a word ends in *e*, only add *-r* or *-st* to the word. Write the appropriate ending in each blank.

8. The ostrich is large____ than most birds.

9. It is probably the tall____ of all birds.

10. Ostrich eggs are the large____ eggs in the world.

11. Its powerful legs make it the fast____ bird on the ground.

The Story of Soap

sequencing

Read "The Story of Soap." Then, write the answers to the questions on the lines below.

Soap has been around for a long time. Babylonians were the first known culture to use soap. They lived more than 4,000 years ago. Babylonians made soap by mixing water, alkali, and cassia oil together.

In the late 19th century, manufactured soap bars became available in Europe and the United States. The advertising campaigns used by the manufacturers to sell their soaps helped increase public awareness of the importance of good hygiene and its relationship to good health.

By the 1950s, soap had become an important instrument for personal hygiene. Today, soap is used for cleaning clothes, dishes, cars, floors, and so much more.

1. What was the first known culture to use soap?

____

2. Where were manufactured soap bars first available?

____

3. Why is good hygiene important?

____

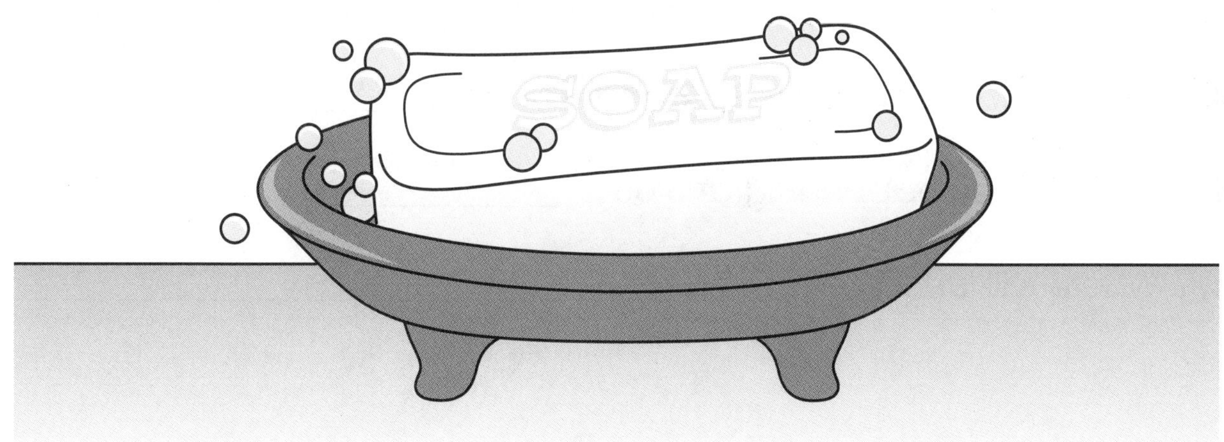

Animal World

Sequence is the order in which a set of events happen. Sequencing provides order and helps you make sense of what you read.

A schedule helps you see the order of events more clearly. Use the schedule below to answer the questions.

Our Day at Animal World	
10:45–11:15	The Reptile Review
11:20–11:45	Elsie the Elephant Show
11:45–12:15	Lunch at the Penguin Palace
12:30–1:00	Sea Lion Show
1:10–1:45	Birds of Prey
2:00–4:45	The Monkey Movie
5:00–6:00	Dinner at the Coyote Café
6:10–6:25	Wildcat Wackiness
6:30–7:00	Penguins on Parade

1. Which show is after the Sea Lion Show? ______________________

2. Is lunch before or after the Elephant Show? ______________________

3. Which shows are after dinner?

   ______________________ and ______________________

4. Which show is before the Elephant Show? ______________________

5. What will be happening at 3:00? ______________________

6. Where will lunch be? ______________________

Key Words

Key words are often used to provide the reader clues about the sequence of a story's events. Words like *first, then, next,* and *last* are examples of key words.

Use the key words to decide which sentence in each pair comes first. Label the sentences **1** and **2**. Then, underline the key words that helped you decide.

1. ____ Before, I walked to school.
   ____ Now, I take the bus to school.

2. ____ Football practice starts soon.
   ____ School starts immediately.

3. ____ First, you need to clean your room.
   ____ Next, you need to fold your clothes.

4. ____ She did her math homework earlier.
   ____ She is finally doing her spelling homework.

5. ____ We need to get to swim lessons right away.
   ____ We need to get to piano lessons eventually.

6. ____ My parents said that we will get a puppy someday.
   ____ My parents said that we will get a fish soon.

7. ____ My mom says that I will learn to like asparagus eventually.
   ____ My mom says that I will never learn to like broccoli.

8. ____ My teacher will send my test scores home later this week.
   ____ My teacher will send my report card home today.

The Midnight Ride

sequencing

Number the sentences from 1-6 to retell the story below in sequence.

It was early morning on April 19, 1775. Paul Revere and many other colonists were ready to fight against the British army. They called themselves *minutemen* because they would need to be ready to fight at a minute's notice. First, Paul waited for a signal from the American spies. They knew the British army would eventually move toward Lexington and Concord, but they did not know whether the British would travel by land or across the water. When the spies told Paul, he would send a signal to the other minutemen, telling them from which direction the British were attacking. Next, he would ride his horse quickly through the farmland and towns, shouting the news that the British were coming.

At last, the word came from the spies. Paul immediately ordered two lanterns to be hung in the tall tower of the church, a signal that meant the British were attacking by sea. Then, he mounted his horse and rode fast into the night. Paul Revere knew the importance of warning the minutemen to prepare for battle. The British army had more men and more guns, so the minutemen would need to surprise them. Paul rode through Lexington, shouting the news. But, as he rode out of town, he was caught by the British. Meanwhile, two other riders made it further and told the minutemen to be ready to fight in Concord.

Soon, the British army reached Concord. They had no idea that the minutemen were waiting. They were surprised and fled the area. The minutemen that were awakened had won their first fight.

____ Paul Revere was caught by a British soldier.

____ Two lanterns were lit in the church tower.

____ Paul Revere rode through Lexington.

____ The minutemen surprised the British army in Concord.

____ Paul Revere received word from the spies.

____ Two other American riders warned the minutemen to gather in Concord.

Air Paths

Unlike stories, directions have no plot. Instead, they help readers do something or get somewhere. Directions should be read one at a time and followed exactly. It might be easy to lose your place or skip important parts. To prevent this, check off the directions as you complete them.

Use the chart below to follow the course of two airplanes as they carry travelers around the United States. Use a red marker to show the path of the Air America plane. Use a blue marker to show the path of the Nations Air plane.

	Left from	1st Stop	2nd Stop	3rd Stop	4th Stop	5th Stop	6th Stop
Air America	Utah (UT)	Colorado (CO)	Texas (TX)	Louisiana (LA)	Tennessee (TN)	Virginia (VA)	Florida (FL)
Nations Air	Michigan (MI)	New York (NY)	Maryland (MD)	Georgia (GA)	Louisiana (LA)	Kansas (KS)	Arizona (AZ)

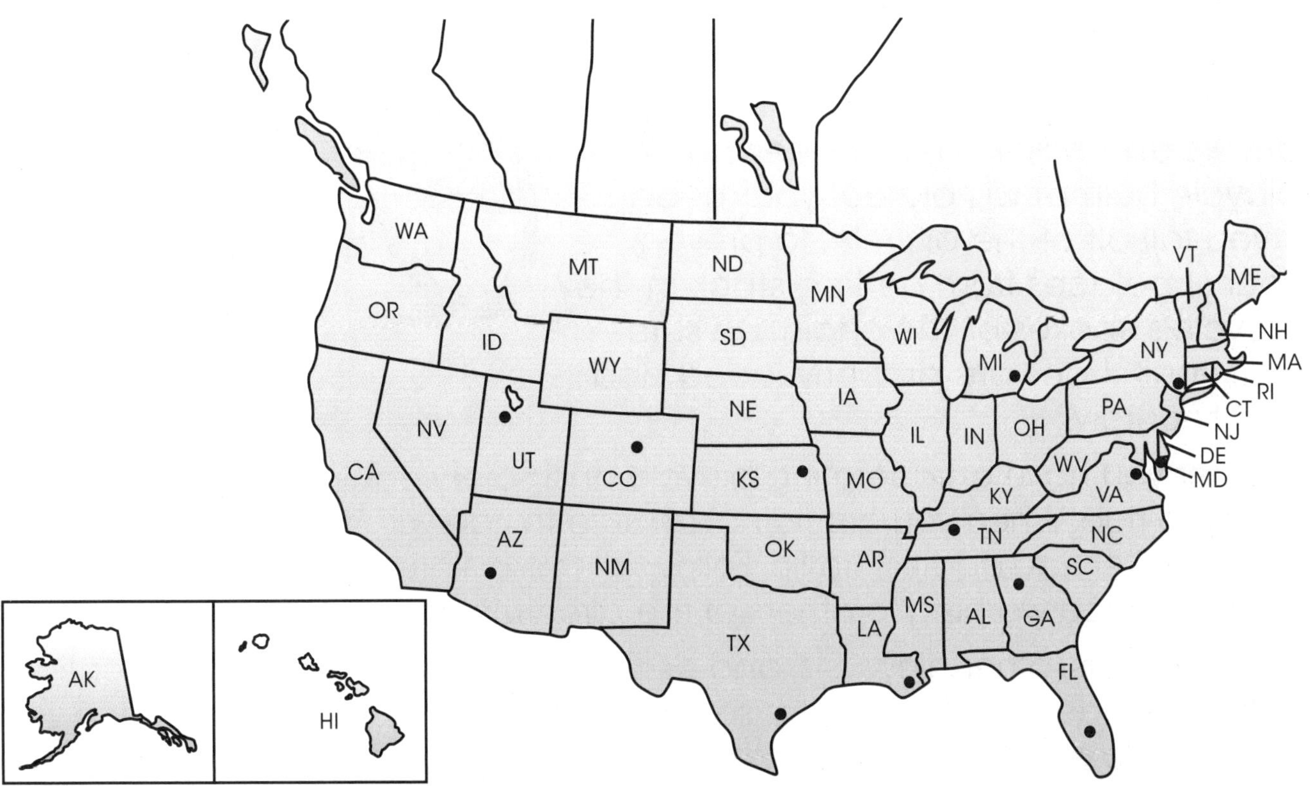

Bicycle Safety

following directions

Read the passage below.

Many people have been hurt while enjoying bicycle rides. Bicycle accidents can be very serious. It is important to learn the safety rules of owning and riding a bicycle. These safety rules are so important that some schools and communities offer bicycle safety courses.

It is important that your bicycle is in good condition before you ride. The tires should have good tread and the correct air pressure. The brakes, the handlebars, and the pedals should all function correctly. If any of these parts do not operate correctly, do not ride the bicycle. You should fix the bicycle first.

After checking your bicycle, make sure that you have the right safety equipment. Reflectors, a bicycle helmet, bright clothing, and laced shoes are important safety requirements to ride a bicycle.

Reflectors and bright clothing help drivers and other riders to see you. A bicycle helmet will protect your head if you fall off of the bicycle. To prevent your shoelaces from getting stuck in the bicycle's spokes or the chain, be sure that your shoes are properly laced and tied securely.

After you have an operating bicycle and safety equipment, you are ready to ride. When you are riding, be sure to ride with the direction of traffic. Never ride against traffic. Follow all traffic signs. Use arm signals to give advance warning to others of the direction you are turning.

Car drivers, other bicyclists, and pedestrians don't always pay attention to bicycle riders. That is why it is so important for bicycle riders to pay attention to everything around them and to follow bicycle safety tips. A safe rider is a happy rider. Have fun!

Bicycle Safety

After reading "Bicycle Safety," answer the following questions.

1. Why is it important to obey bicycle safety rules?

____

2. When should you wear bright clothing?

A. during the day
B. during the evening
C. every time you ride
D. never

3. What parts on the bicycle should you check before riding?

____

4. What safety equipment should you use when you ride?

____

5. On which side of the street should you ride your bike?

A. with the direction of traffic
B. the left side
C. on the sidewalk
D. doesn't matter where

U.S. Presidents

Classifying means putting things in groups. One way to group things is to look for similarities. For example, you can group things by days, months, or years. History books are often classified by time.

The names of several American presidents are written below. Classify them by the years they began their terms as president.

1901–T. Roosevelt	1974–G. Ford	1945–H. Truman
1885–G. Cleveland	2001–G. W. Bush	1817–J. Monroe
1993–W. Clinton	1789–G. Washington	1861–A. Lincoln
1797–J. Adams	1845–J. Polk	1801–T. Jefferson
1837–M. Van Buren	1869–U. Grant	1981–R. Reagan
1913–W. Wilson	1961–J. Kennedy	1929–H. Hoover

1789–1799

1. ____________________

2. ____________________

1800–1849

1. ____________________

2. ____________________

3. ____________________

4. ____________________

1850–1899

1. ____________________

2. ____________________

3. ____________________

1900–1949

1. ____________________

2. ____________________

3. ____________________

4. ____________________

1950–1999

1. ____________________

2. ____________________

3. ____________________

4. ____________________

2000–2007

1. ____________________

Which Word Does Not Belong?

When you look for the item that does not belong in a group, try to find what the others have in common.

Example: star, moon, rocket, planet
The rocket does not fit because it is not a natural part of space.

Cross out the word that does not belong in each group.

1.	2.	3.	4.
boot sandal sock sneaker	Uranus Orion Big Dipper Little Dipper	paper clip glue orange tape	celery lettuce apple broccoli
5.	**6.**	**7.**	**8.**
catfish tuna salmon dolphin	pink yellow blue red	candle mirror flashlight lantern	heart green leprechaun clover
9.	**10.**	**11.**	**12.**
ears eyes nose arm	stairs pit mountain ladder	shirt socks pants window	book magazine baseball menu

Extra!
Write the names of 12 items that are in your closet. Then, classify them into groups.

Animal Poem

Read the poem below.

How many animals can you name?
This seems like a never-ending game.

There are little ants so very small.
There are spotted giraffes so very tall.

There are mammals and insects to name a few.
There are reptiles and amphibians in the zoo.

There are animals that fly and some that walk.
There are cows in a herd and birds in a flock.

There are animals on land and at sea.
There are animals in the ground and some in trees.

There are animals that are wild and some that are tame.
There are too many animals for us to ever name!

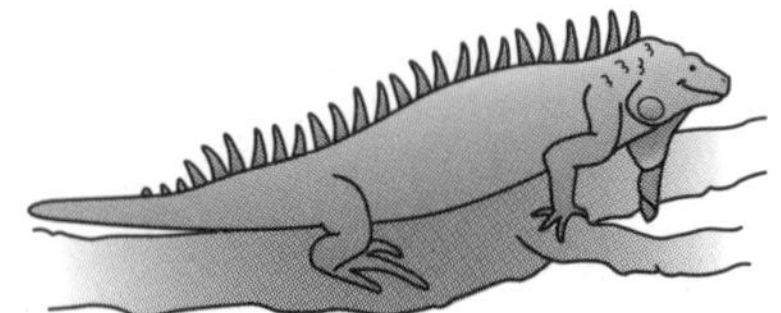

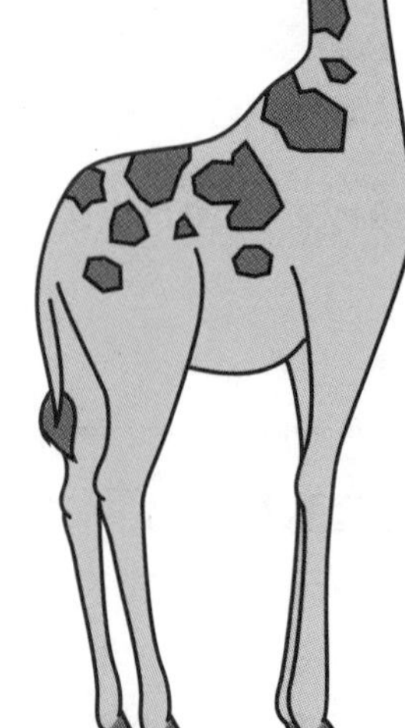

Animal Poem

1. What is the main idea of the poem?
   - **A.** There are too many animals to name.
   - **B.** Animals make great pets.
   - **C.** Some animals are wild, and some are tame.

2. Three animals that are mentioned by name in the poem are
   - **A.** giraffes, ants, and cows.
   - **B.** sea animals, cows, and ants.
   - **C.** sea turtles, crows, and ants.

3. Draw a line between antonyms.

land	tame
ground	sky
wild	tall
few	sea
small	many

4. Find five plural nouns in the poem. Write them on the lines.

____

____

____

____

____

____

____

Cross out the animal that does not belong in each group.

5.	hawk whale	owl robin
6.	horse sheep	cow giraffe
7.	squirrel dog	monkey koala
8.	snake cricket	ant grasshopper
9.	tiger rabbit	lion leopard

In a Neighborly Way

Characters are people, animals, or animated objects in stories. The most important characters are called *main characters*. They are brought to life by their actions. You may witness a character's personality change as a story unfolds.

Read the story below. Then, answer the questions.

Casey was excited to meet his new neighbors. They had a son who looked about Casey's age. It did not take long for the boys to become friendly, and soon Casey asked his new neighbor, Nick, to play at his house. The boys spent the first hour playing the games that Nick chose. Casey did not mind, because he knew it was polite to let the guest choose. After another half hour, Casey thought it should be his turn to choose a game.

"No, I don't want to," Nick stubbornly replied.

"But, I haven't chosen a game yet," Casey said.

"Well, if you won't play what I want, I'm going home," Nick threatened.

Casey did not want his new friend to leave, so he agreed to play Nick's chosen game.

The next time Casey's mom offered to invite Nick over, Casey declined. He told his mom how selfishly Nick had acted before. His mom offered an idea.

Nick came over that afternoon. It was not long before he threatened to leave again. This time, Casey said, "Okay, you can go home. I really wanted to be friends, but I want friends who are fair. I'll see you later."

Nick could not believe his ears! Would his new friend really let him leave? He thought about the way he had acted and said, "I'm sorry. Let's play the game you choose now. I want to be a fair friend."

1. Write two words to describe Casey.

   A. ______________________ **B.** ______________________

2. Write two words to describe Nick at the beginning of the story.

   A. ______________________ **B.** ______________________

3. Write two words to describe Nick at the end of the story.

   A. ______________________ **B.** ______________________

Dear Donna

June 13, 2006

Dear Donna,

The other day was a bad day for my mom and me. I forgot to pick a few ears of corn from our garden for dinner, and she was upset. She even *restricted* me from playing outside. I can understand why she was so upset with me; I forgot to do my chores.

A few hours after she sent me to my room, I apologized to her for forgetting. I think my apology made my mom feel better, because she let me go outside to play. I was excited to use the new kite that I got for my birthday.

The sun was shining brightly, and there was just enough wind to fly my kite. After I looked at the kite flying high up in the sky, a feeling of happiness came over me. It was like magic!

The wind started to die down, so I decided to pull my kite down and go home. The minute I walked into the kitchen holding my kite, my mom smiled at me. I asked her why she was smiling. Mom told me that my red cheeks and the smile on my face made her happy!

After dinner, I went to my mom and kissed her on the cheek. She asked me why I did that. I told her that her smile made me happy. It was a good ending to a bad day. I hope to hear from you soon.

Your best friend,

Ebony

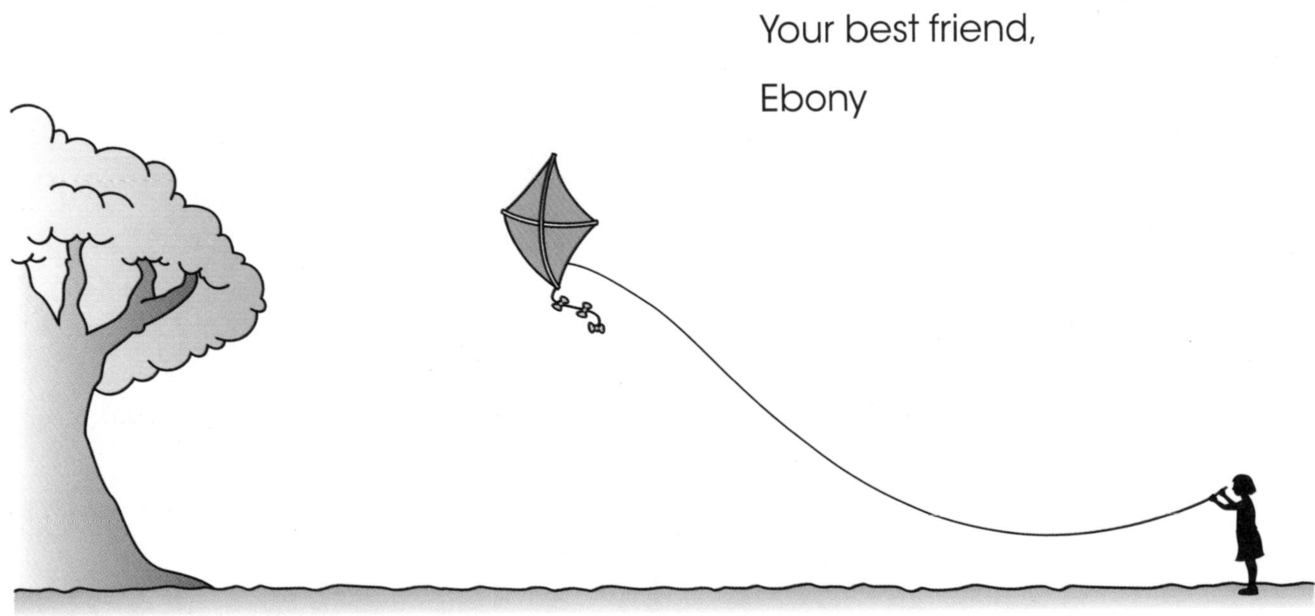

Dear Donna

After reading "Dear Donna," answer the following questions.

1. The word *restricted* means
   - **A.** vacationed
   - **B.** confined
   - **C.** worked
   - **D.** played

2. What was Ebony's punishment for not completing her chore?
   - **A.** cleaning her room
   - **B.** flying a kite
   - **C.** not playing outside
   - **D.** cleaning the dishes

3. What feeling did Ebony get when she was able to fly her kite?
   - **A.** happy
   - **B.** depressed
   - **C.** anxious
   - **D.** scared

4. What made Ebony's mother happy?
   - **A.** dinner
   - **B.** Ebony's red cheeks and smile
   - **C.** Ebony's kite
   - **D.** gardening

5. Why do you think Ebony likes to see her mother smile?

____

____

____

____

____

Finding the Cause

Many stories add a cause and effect to help the reader understand why something has happened. Think about "Little Red Riding Hood."

Effect (what happened):
Little Red Riding Hood thought her grandma looked strange.

Cause (what made it happen):
It was really the wolf dressed up!

For each effect below, find the cause and write the letter on the line.

____ **1.** When her mom called her for dinner, she almost felt sick. "I cannot eat a thing," she said.

____ **2.** The house was a mess! Magazines and newspapers had been torn to pieces, and the bag of dog food was spilled all over the kitchen floor.

____ **3.** The team had finished warming up, and it was time for the game to begin. "How can we start without our pitcher?" the team wondered. "Where is he?"

____ **4.** We would have to drive more slowly than we expected.

A. As we approached the shore, the fog became so thick that we could hardly see in front of us. Mom turned on the lights and told us to settle in.

B. Jamie's mom was not around when she got home from school. Jamie helped herself to a handful of pretzels and a bowl of ice cream. Then, she found the cookies her mom had baked.

C. Billy promised to go straight home after school to take care of his dog. Then, Billy's neighbor invited him to play a quick game of basketball on their way home. "Okay," he agreed.

D. "Mom, can I spend the night at Chase's house?" Carlos asked. "Carlos, you have an early game tomorrow," she answered. "That's okay, Mom, I won't be too tired," Carlos begged.

Stray Cat Hero

cause and effect

My mom always takes in stray animals. The one I remember best was a mangy kitten.

One day, a dirty, hungry little kitten wandered onto our porch. Mom took pity on the kitten. She brought it in the house, gave it a bath, and fed it. She took special care of this kitten.

One night, we were all sound asleep. At about two in the morning, I heard loud meowing. Mom's stray kitten jumped next to my face and began to lick me. I pushed the cat away, rolled over, and went back to sleep. The persistent cat wouldn't take no for an answer. He went to my dad. My dad pushed the cat over to my mom's side of the bed. Although my mom is a very heavy sleeper, the cat continued to meow and lick her face. Finally, my mom awoke. At first, she was annoyed. But, then she realized what the cat wanted. Mom smelled gas. She immediately woke Dad. They turned the gas off and opened all of the windows. We had a gas leak that no one noticed except our stray cat. Mom's stray cat had saved us. That's how the little stray kitten became our family pet, and that's how Hero got his name!

Stray Cat Hero

1. Number the sentences in the order that they happened in the story.

____ Mom took care of a stray cat.
____ We named the stray cat Hero.
____ The cat tried to wake Dad.
____ The cat woke Mom.
____ Mom smelled gas.
____ Mom and Dad turned off the gas.

Cause is why something happens. **Effect** is the event that happens. Circle the correct answer below.

2. Because Hero woke Mom,
   - **A.** she got scratched.
   - **B.** she smelled the gas.
   - **C.** the family awoke.
3. They opened all of the windows
   - **A.** to let Hero outside.
   - **B.** because they were hot.
   - **C.** because there was a gas smell.
4. Mom gave the kitten a bath
   - **A.** because no one else would.
   - **B.** because it asked her to.
   - **C.** because it was dirty and she felt pity for it.

Draw a line between the present tense and past tense of each word.

5.	take	brought
6.	become	went
7.	bring	began
8.	begin	took
9.	go	became

10. What is a stray animal?
    - **A.** a dangerous animal
    - **B.** a dirty animal
    - **C.** an animal without a home
11. Someone who is persistent
    - **A.** doesn't give up.
    - **B.** is very loud.
    - **C.** can smell very well.

Some sentences can be combined using the word *and.* Use the word *and* to combine the sentences below. Rewrite them on the lines provided.

12. Our cat smelled gas. He tried to wake us.

____
____
____

13. Mom takes in stray animals. She gives them baths.

____
____
____

A New Zealand Treat

Read the recipe below. Then, answer the questions on page 55.

New Zealand's Pavlova

Ingredients:

½ tsp. salt
3 egg whites
¾ tsp. vanilla
¼ tsp. cream of tartar
¾ c. caster sugar*
1 compass

Equipment:

1 baking sheet
1 wooden spoon
1 egg separator
1 small mixing bowl
2 airtight containers
black pen
measuring cups
measuring spoons
wax paper
electric mixer

* Caster sugar is a very fine sugar from New Zealand. You can find it in specialty shops. Powdered sugar may be substituted.

1. Preheat the oven to 300°F.

2. Place the egg separator over the mixing bowl. Carefully crack one egg into the separator. The egg yolk will stay in the separator. The egg white will fall into the bowl. Pour the yolk into an airtight container. Crack two more eggs in the same way.

3. Set the egg whites aside at room temperature for one half hour. Save the egg yolks to use another time. Put them in the refrigerator.

4. Tear off a sheet of wax paper the same size as the baking sheet. Draw 12 three-inch circles onto the wax paper. An easy way to do this is to use a compass. From the center point of a circle, measure out $1\frac{1}{2}$ inches. That will create a three-inch circle. Turn the wax paper so that the writing side faces down. Place the paper on the baking sheet.

5. Add vanilla, cream of tartar, and salt to the egg whites. Beat with an electric mixer on high speed. Do this until soft peaks form. Be sure to have an adult help you.

6. Add sugar, one tablespoon at a time. Keep beating at high speed until stiff peaks form. The sugar should be almost dissolved. This should take about five minutes. This mixture is called *meringue*.

7. Put equal spoonfuls of meringue onto each circle. Use all of the mixture. Shape the meringue to make bowls.

8. Bake in the oven for 35 minutes. Then, turn off the oven and let the bowls dry for one hour. Carefully pull each bowl off of the wax paper. Store them in an airtight container.

Filling:

Pile fresh fruit, such as peaches or strawberries, into each shell. Top with dairy whipped topping. Drizzle a small amount of fruit sauce on top of each bowl.

A New Zealand Treat

Cause is why something happens. **Effect** is the event that happens. Circle each correct cause.

1. The egg white will fall into the bowl
   - **A.** when it reaches room temperature.
   - **B.** if the separator catches it.
   - **C.** if you crack the egg over the egg separator.
2. Stiff peaks will form
   - **A.** when the cook gets angry.
   - **B.** when you have beaten the egg white mixture long enough.
   - **C.** if the room is cold.
3. The meringue bowls will not stick to the baking sheet
   - **A.** if you use wax paper.
   - **B.** if they are pulled off fast enough.
   - **C.** because there is no glue in the recipe.

A **glossary** gives the meaning of special words or phrases used in a book. Use the following glossary to answer the questions. Write the correct word for each meaning on the lines provided.

c., cup (noun)
1. A cup measure or eight ounces of an ingredient.

cream of tartar (noun)
1. An ingredient found in the spice section of the grocery store.

drizzle (verb)
1. To lightly sprinkle with a liquid topping.

ingredient (noun)
1. An item of food used in a recipe.

meringue (noun)
1. A baked mixture of sugar and stiffly beaten egg whites.

preheat (verb)
1. To heat an oven ahead of time.

soft peak (noun)
1. noun A high point that curves to one side.

stiff peak (noun)
1. A high point that is not bent over.

tsp., teaspoon (noun)
1. A small spoon used to measure an ingredient.

4. To heat an oven before you are ready to bake

   ____

5. When a beaten mixture looks like a mountain top gently curving to one side

   ____

6. An ingredient found in the spice section

   ____

7. A small spoon used to measure an ingredient

   ____

8. To lightly sprinkle with a liquid topping

   ____

American Indian Dance

Informational passages are written to teach something. In them, you may find facts, opinions, or a mix of both.

Read the passage below.

Dancing is a valued tradition among several American Indian tribes. American Indians dance for many different reasons. Their dances are very exciting. They dance for birthdays and marriage ceremonies. The dances are beautiful and graceful. Dancing is not only for special occasions. American Indians also dance powwows. Powwows are dances they have for fun. Dancers usually move in a circle. By dancing in a circle, tribes are able to stay symbolically connected to their family and traditions. American Indian dances are the best in the world.

Write three facts from the passage.

1. ______________________________

2. ______________________________

3. ______________________________

Write three opinions from the passage.

4. ______________________________

5. ______________________________

6. ______________________________

Sea Horses

fact or opinion

Read the passage below.

Sea horses are interesting creatures for many reasons. Their scientific name is *Hippocampus*. It comes from two Greek words: *hippos*, which means "horse" and *kampos*, which means "sea monster." To survive in the ocean, sea horses live in environments that camouflage them from predators. Sea horses range in size from 6 to 12 inches, although most are about 6 inches long. They can be many colors, including white, yellow, red, brown, black, and gray, with spots or stripes. However, the most interesting thing about sea horses is that they put a *twist* in parenting. Instead of females carrying the young, males carry them!

A male sea horse has a pouch on his underside where he carries eggs. The female sea horse places her eggs into the male's pouch. Then, the male sea horse carries the eggs for about 21 days until they hatch. The female sea horse visits the male sea horse every morning until the babies are born. Newborn sea horses rise to the surface of the water and take a gulp of air, which helps them stay upright.

When sea horses are born, they feed on tiny sea creatures, using their snouts. They are able to swim, but sometimes they get washed up onshore by storms or eaten by fish, crabs, or water birds.

A few days after giving birth, the male joins the female again. Within hours, he has a new sack full of eggs. This is the life cycle of the sea horse. Sea horses are indeed interesting animals!

Sea Horses

After reading "Sea Horses," answer the following questions.

1. What do newborn sea horses usually eat?

   A. crabs
   B. flowers
   C. tiny sea animals
   D. sand

2. Why do you think the author used the word *twist* in the first paragraph?

   ____

   ____

3. Why do newborn sea horses rise to the surface of the water?

   ____

   ____

4. What word means "sea monster"?

   A. kampos
   B. phylum
   C. hippos
   D. genus

5. In your opinion, what is the most interesting thing about the sea horse?

   ____

   ____

   ____

   ____

Eight Minutes Over France

drawing conclusions

Do you like to travel in different ways? Then try going by hot air balloon. The idea existed for 2,000 years. But, it took the king of France, two brothers, a sheep, a duck, and a chicken to make it happen.

The king of France thought a person would die traveling by balloon. So, two brothers did a test. They sent the three animals up in a basket attached to a balloon.

The animals flew over France for eight minutes. The king was excited when they returned safely. Two months later, a major in the army and a physics professor went up in a balloon.

A hot air balloon is so simple, anyone could fly one. Turning a knob lets gas into the balloon. This makes the balloon go up. Pulling a cord changes the amount of gas and makes the balloon rise quickly or slowly. If the cord lets enough gas out, the balloon sinks. The wind moves the balloon from place to place.

In the 1960s, hot air balloons became very popular. A man named Ed Yost worked with Raven Industries to design and make hot air balloons. Then, the United States Navy asked Ed's company to help them. The Navy wanted to use balloons to send packages.

Ed Yost and the Navy made important changes. Balloons were made from a new material. The balloon's shape was made to look like a giant light bulb.

Someone also invented a new way to inflate the balloon. Now just the top part of the balloon is filled. Some safety changes were also made. It is safer than ever to travel by hot air balloon.

After a while, the Navy lost interest in hot air balloons. But Ed Yost didn't give up. He sold hot air balloons for sports events.

Hot air balloon businesses make millions of dollars. Balloon races attract crowds of watchers. Many people take part in the fun.

Everyone should ride in a hot air balloon! Some people have traveled around the world in balloons. Once you try it, you will never want to fly any other way.

Eight Minutes Over France

If something can be proven, it is a fact. If something can't be proven, it is an opinion. Circle *F* for fact or *O* for opinion.

1. The king was excited when the animals returned safely.
   F O
2. A hot air balloon is so simple, anyone can fly one.
   F O
3. It is safer than ever to travel by hot air balloon.
   F O
4. Everyone should ride in a hot air balloon.
   F O

You can often guess what a word means by looking at the words around it. Read the passage to circle each correct answer.

5. The word *sink* means
   - **A.** to go toward the ground.
   - **B.** to rise up slowly.
   - **C.** a place to wash your hands.

6. The word *inflate* means
   - **A.** a new idea.
   - **B.** to fill something with air.
   - **C.** a safety change.

A **compound subject** is two or more nouns connected by the word *and*. Underline the compound subject in each sentence.

7. The king of France and two brothers made it happen.
8. A major in the army and a physics professor went up.
9. Ed Yost and Raven Industries began to design hot air balloons.
10. Ed Yost and the Navy made important changes.

Irregular verbs do not add *-ed* to make the past tense. They change their form. Write the present tense of each bold verb.

11. The king of France **thought** a man would die up in a balloon. ________________
12. So, two brothers **did** a test.
    ____
13. Ed Yost and Raven Industries **began** to design hot air balloons. ________________
14. He **sold** hot air balloons for sports events. ________________

What Happens?

Drawing conclusions means using the information in a story to make a logical guess.

Read each passage. Circle the letter for each sentence that is a reasonable conclusion. Some passages have more than one answer.

1. Minnie was glad to be home after two hours of ballet practice. She could hear crickets in the woods outside her window as she turned to chapter four in her book. As she finished the chapter, she pulled the covers back to turn off the light. She burst into laughter when she looked down and realized what she was wearing.

- **A.** Minnie forgot to take off her dance tutu.
- **B.** Minnie had already washed her face.
- **C.** Minnie stayed up past her bedtime.
- **D.** Minnie had read part of the book before.

2. Murphy's mom quickly pulled everything out of the dryer. Then, she lifted the lid of the washer, looked inside, and shook her head. She looked around the kitchen and family room, then she rushed upstairs. "I cannot find them," she called to Murphy. "The last time I saw them was after your game on Saturday. We have to find them before 4:00!"

- **A.** Murphy's mom has friends coming over at 4:00.
- **B.** Murphy's mom is looking for Murphy's football pants.
- **C.** Murphy has a game today at 4:00.
- **D.** Murphy's mom lost her purse.

3. Tia walked slowly to the end of the board and looked down at the water. She wanted to jump, but her feet would not cooperate. She turned and walked back, then climbed down the ladder. "Next time," she told herself.

- **A.** Tia's friends can jump off the diving board.
- **B.** Tia is swimming.
- **C.** Tia wants to jump.
- **D.** Tia is nervous.

Miss Nelson

In the book *Miss Nelson Is Missing!*, by Harry Allard (Houghton Mifflin Company, 1977) a classroom teacher must help her students learn a lesson about manners, and she uses a creative approach.

Watch for clues as you read the summary below.

The students in Miss Nelson's class were misbehaving again. They were making spitballs and paper airplanes, rather than listening as Miss Nelson read during story hour. "Something will have to be done," Miss Nelson said to herself.

The next day, Miss Nelson was not at school. The students planned to misbehave worse than ever as they heard footsteps approaching the door. But, they were horrified to meet their new substitute teacher, Miss Viola Swamp. She wore an ugly black dress and spoke in a nasty voice. The students were afraid and did exactly as they were told.

After a few days, the students missed Miss Nelson. They were beginning to think that they would be stuck with Miss Swamp forever. Then, one morning they heard footsteps approaching their door, and they were pleasantly surprised to see Miss Nelson! During story hour that day, no one misbehaved. There were no more spitballs or paper airplanes.

That evening, Miss Nelson went home and giggled as she saw the ugly black dress hanging in her closet.

Which of these conclusions can you make based on the clues in the story? Write *yes* or *no* next to each sentence.

_____ **1.** Miss Nelson was sick.

_____ **2.** Miss Nelson is a kind teacher.

_____ **3.** Miss Swamp is really Miss Nelson.

_____ **4.** Miss Swamp has a sister.

_____ **5.** The students in Miss Nelson's class behave now.

_____ **6.** The students in Miss Nelson's class miss Miss Swamp.

_____ **7.** Miss Nelson will never miss school again.

Mammals or Birds?

drawing conclusions

> When you read to find information, similarities and differences can help you learn more.

Bats are amazing animals. They have ears and noses like other mammals, but they have wings like birds. Or do they? Scientists have found that a bat's wing bones are like human hands. A bat has a thumb and four fingers that form each wing. The wings are not covered in feathers, but with a thick skin. Baby bats are born alive and drink milk from their mothers, like all mammals. So, are they mammals or birds?

To help you decide whether bats are mammals or birds, make a list of similarities and differences below.

Bats and Mammals

Alike: ______________________

____

____

____

Different: ______________________

____

____

____

Bats and Birds

Alike: ______________________

____

____

____

Different: ______________________

____

____

____

What have you concluded? Is a bat a bird or mammal? Why?

____

____

Who's Prince Charming?

Read the story below. Then, answer the questions on page 65.

With the help of her fairy godmother, Cinderella makes it to the ball. However, when she arrives she is greeted by five handsome gentlemen. At first, Cinderella becomes upset. She is afraid she will never find the right prince! Then, she remembers the handbook her fairy godmother gave her. She pulls it from her purse and begins reading. Use the clues in the handbook to help Cinderella find her Prince Charming.

How to Tell a Real Prince from a Fake

1. A real prince always wears a crown.
2. A real prince always wears a ring on his right hand.
3. A real prince never wears a wristwatch.
4. A real prince never wears sneakers.
5. A real prince always wears shirts with exactly seven buttons.

Who's Prince Charming?

1. Circle the real Prince Charming on page 64.

2. Write a *T* next to the sentences that are true. Write an *F* next to the sentences that are false.

____ The fairy godmother helped Cinderella get to the ball.

____ The fairy godmother gave Cinderella a handbook.

____ The real prince wears a wristwatch.

____ The real prince wears sneakers.

____ The real prince wears a ring on his right hand and a crown.

Draw a line between the two words that make up each compound word.

3. gentlemen
4. horseshoe
5. handbook
6. godmother
7. wristwatch

8. What else do you think might have been in the handbook the fairy godmother gave to Cinderella?

____

____

____

Underline the verb, circle the subject, and mark an *X* on the object in each sentence.

9. The prince's shirt has exactly seven buttons.
10. The prince is wearing a crown.
11. Cinderella read the book.

An **antonym** is a word that means the opposite of another word. Write an antonym of each bold word.

12. The princes were **handsome**.

    ____

13. Cinderella becomes **upset**.

    ____

14. She fears she will never **find** her prince.

    ____

15. Do you think Cinderella will **remember** her handbook?

    ____

The Snow Child

Many years ago, there lived a woman and a man. As they grew older, they also grew sadder, for they had no children. One winter morning, the man looked out the window at the falling snow. "Let's build a snow child," he suggested to his wife. "Yes," said the woman, "a snow child just for us."

The man and the woman went outside and began to make a little girl out of snow. They made her legs, her arms, and her head. They used bits of sparkling blue ice for her eyes. When the man and woman finished, they stood back to look at what they had created. They could hardly believe their eyes. They had created a beautiful snow child. The woman kissed the snow child gently on the cheek. Suddenly, the snow child began to smile. She stretched out her arms. She stretched out her legs. She spun around and gave a little laugh. "I'm alive," she giggled with delight. Then, she ran and gave the old man and the woman a hug. Nothing could have made the couple happier. At last, they had the child they longed for.

The days passed. Soon, the winter storms turned to spring showers. The sun began to warm the earth. The signs of spring were everywhere. But, as the days became warmer, the snow child became more and more unhappy. She would not go outside. "Come, little daughter. Why do you look so sad? Go outside and play with the other children," said the woman. The snow child did as she was told.

But before the snow child could join the other children, she disappeared. There was only a white mist where the girl had stood. The mist formed into a thin cloud and rose higher and higher, until it joined the clouds in the sky. The man and the woman wept bitterly at the loss of their dear little snow child. Once again, they were sad and lonely.

After many months, the days became shorter and the nights longer. The air was crisp and cool once again. Winter was coming. One night, as the first snow began to fall, the couple sat by the window remembering their dear little snow child. Suddenly, they heard a happy laugh and a familiar voice singing,

Winter is here. I am back with the snow. Do not fear, when comes spring I go. I will return with the snow each year, for you, my parents, are oh, so dear.

The couple ran to the door. They hugged their little snow child. How happy they were to be together again! The snow child stayed with them through each winter. Then, when spring came, she disappeared until winter returned to the couple's cottage again.

The Snow Child

1. Why were the man and the woman sad at the beginning of the story?
   - **A.** because they were growing old
   - **B.** because they had no children
   - **C.** because the winter was too cold

2. What brought the snow child to life?
   - **A.** a fairy godmother
   - **B.** a snowflake
   - **C.** the woman's kiss

The ending *-er* often means "more." Sometimes, it is used to compare two things. The ending *-est* means "most." It is used to compare more than two things. Write the correct word to complete each sentence.

3. The days are getting ________ now that summer is here.
4. That clown looks __________ than the one with the frown on his face.
5. Jessie's hair is ____________ than Claudia's.
6. Ilene is three years ________ than Kevin.
7. That statue is ____________ on the shelf than I thought.

Write the base word for each word below. On another sheet of paper, add *-est* to each word and use it in a sentence.

8. warmer ________________
9. happier ________________
10. shorter ________________
11. older ________________
12. higher ________________

13. Why would the snow child disappear in the spring?

    ____

    ____

    ____

14. In the story, what are some signs of spring?

    ____

    ____

    ____

15. In the story, what are some signs of winter?

    ____

    ____

    ____

Ellen's Helpers

predicting outcomes

You can predict what could happen next by using the clues within a story.

Circle the letter of the sentence that tells what will probably happen next.

1. Ellen was excited to spend the morning at the park with her mother and her three-year-old twin brothers, Sam and Adam. Ellen offered to start packing their lunches while her mom got the boys ready to go. It was not long before Sam appeared at Ellen's feet and asked to help. Ellen explained that she was in a hurry to get to the park. Sam turned to the refrigerator and took out the grapes. The bowl was much too big for him to hold, and . . .

A. Sam put the grapes in the lunch basket.
B. Sam dropped the bowl.
C. Sam ate all of the grapes.

2. Grapes went everywhere. At that moment, Adam ran into the room and slid on the grapes. Ellen grabbed the broom while her mom settled the boys in another room. As Ellen and her mom finished sweeping the floor, they heard a loud crash in the broom closet. When they went to look, they saw Sam and Adam standing in the closet with the vacuum in their hands. They wanted to help clean up the grapes, but the vacuum had fallen to the floor. The dust bag had broken open, and the boys were . . .

A. sitting in a pile of dust.
B. playing with their blocks.
C. laughing at a movie.

3. Ellen and her mother quickly cleaned the boys and headed for the car. "Oh, no," said Ellen's mom. "I forgot to feed the dog." Hearing this, . . .

A. Sam and Adam jumped into their car seats.
B. Sam and Adam asked for a snack.
C. Sam and Adam ran toward the big bag of dog food.

The Musicians of Bremen

predicting outcomes

Make predictions as you come to questions. Do not read ahead!

Long ago, there lived a donkey who faithfully served his master for many years. The donkey had become too old to carry sacks of grain, and his master planned to do away with him. The donkey developed a plan to run away to the town of Bremen, where he would become a musician. The donkey had not gone too far when he came upon an old hunting dog lying on the ground. The dog explained that he had become too old to hunt any longer, and that his master had plans to get rid of him.

1. What do you think will happen next?______________________________

____

The donkey suggested that the dog join him in Bremen and become a musician. The dog agreed, and the two continued their journey. Farther down the road, they happened upon an old cat and an old rooster, both afraid as well. They decided to join the donkey and the dog. As night fell, the travelers became tired and hungry. They spotted a house in the woods and approached it. Peering in, they saw a table full of food and a band of robbers sitting around it. They screeched out their music as loud as they could, scaring the robbers away.

2. What do you think the four musicians will do now? ______________

____

After the animals fell asleep, the robbers came back to the house. They saw the cat's eyes reflecting light, and began to run. The dog bit their legs, the donkey kicked them, and the rooster crowed. The robbers were so scared they never returned to the house again.

3. What will the animals do now? ______________________________

____

The Ants Go Marching

Read the story below.

Out of the blue, Aunt Cathy started laughing and hiccuping. Then, they sang, "The ants go marching one by one, hurrah, hurrah. The ants go marching one by one, hurrah, hurrah. The ants go marching one by one. The little one stops to have some fun. Then, they all go marching down to the ground to get out of the rain. Boom, boom, boom, boom. Boom, boom, boom, boom."

"Yes, snicker doodle, I remember," Chloe said quickly. She didn't want to hear all 50 verses of that song ever again. They sang and sang, adding more and more verses while it continued to rain. Heather's dad was coming to jump-start the car. It would take three hours to get home, with Heather and Aunt Cathy singing all the way. Chloe kept chiming in, "Put a sock in it." But, they kept singing.

While they waited for Heather's dad, things started to get really exciting. Lightning crashed across the sky. Trees lit up, and birds screeched. With Aunt Cathy hiccuping and Heather singing about ants, Chloe began to get, well, antsy. She said that they couldn't just lollygag all night. The sound of thunder and the flash of lightning were coming closer together.

Suddenly, lightning struck a tree by the river. Aunt Cathy got the hiccups scared right out of her. Heather stopped singing. But, by now Peter was dead to the world, so he missed it all. Luckily, the downpour put out the fire from the lightning. After that, they kept their eyes peeled.

Then, the headlights came at them head-on. They nearly jumped out of their skins. It couldn't be Heather's father. Chloe had just called him on her cell phone....

The Ants Go Marching

The ants go marching one by one,
hurrah, hurrah!

The ants go marching one by one,
hurrah, hurrah!

The ants go marching one by one.

The little one stops to have some fun.

Then, they all go marching down to
the ground to get out of the rain.

Boom, boom, boom, boom!

Boom, boom, boom, boom!

The Ants Go Marching

An **idiom** is a phrase that means something different than what it seems to mean.

1. List three idioms you find in the story on page 70.

   A. ______________________

   B. ______________________

   C. ______________________

Write the matching word from the story for each meaning below.

antsy	little
skin	lollygag

2. small

   ____

3. the outer covering on a body

   ____

4. anxious

   ____

5. to loaf or do nothing

   ____

6. Write your own verse for the song "The Ants Go Marching." To keep the rhythm of the song, follow the pattern of the words in the verse on page 70.

   ____

   ____

   ____

   ____

   ____

   ____

   ____

7. Predict what might happen next in the story. Write your own ending to the chapter.

   ____

   ____

   ____

   ____

   ____

   ____

   ____

What Happened?

To make an **inference** means to make an educated guess using the information given.

Example: *Keisha soaked up the milk with a sponge.*
You can infer from the information that milk was probably spilled.

The sentences below imply that something has happened. Write a sentence for each telling what may have happened.

1. The boy's mom apologized to the shop owner.

 ____

2. The dog sat by the fire to warm himself.

 ____

3. The animals scurried back into the woods.

 ____

4. The boys roared with laughter.

 ____

5. Tasha swung her bat even harder the second time.

 ____

6. Marcus counted the money left in his wallet.

 ____

Dialogue Detectives

Making an inference is like being a detective. You use the information you have to think about what may have happened previously.

Use the dialogue between characters to make an inference. Then, write the next part of the script.

Mom: Hi, Brian. How was school today?

Brian: It was great. Wait until you hear about it. You are going to smile from ear to ear.

Mom: I cannot wait to hear. What happened?

Brian: ______________________________

____

____

____

Dad: Sean, are you awake?

Sean: Wow, I am so tired. I almost fell asleep right here at the baseball game.

Dad: Well, I am not surprised after last night.

Sean: ______________________________

____

____

____

Sandra: What time did Tina say she will be here?

Missy: Right after her soccer game. It should be any minute.

Sandra: I wonder what her big surprise is. She said it definitely involves us.

Missy: She has been very sneaky lately, and I heard her say something about a famous rock group.

Tina: ______________________________

____

The Money Plant

Read the story below.

There was a man who lived on Hills Lane. The children on the street went to visit him every day after school. The man baked cookies for them and taught them how to play games. He loved when they came to visit him.

His favorite hobby was growing plants. He had many different types of plants. The children helped him pull weeds around the plants and give them water. There was one plant that the man thought was dead. He asked the children to throw it away.

As a surprise, the children decided to nurse the plant back to health. Every day after school they crept into the backyard, where they watered and talked to the plant. The man had no idea what the children were doing.

One day, the children noticed that the plant had grown strange green leaves. They were so excited that they ran inside to tell the man about it. When the man went outside, he noticed that the strange little leaves looked just like dollar bills! Could it be that this was a money plant?

The Money Plant

The next morning, the man went to check the plant and found hundreds of dollars on the stems! He pulled the money off, and instantly more bills appeared! He was shocked. He wasn't quite sure what to do. He decided to go inside, eat breakfast, and think about how to use the money.

The man decided to give each of the children some of the money because they had cared for the plant. When the children came over that afternoon, he told them his plan. The children were very excited!

The man divided the money among the children, and they ran to their homes to share the news. The next day, the man made a special batch of cookies for his friends. He waited and waited, but they never came to visit. He thought they were out spending their money and would come to visit the next day. The next day came and went, and the children never visited. This made the man very sad.

He went outside to the backyard and pulled the money plant up by the roots. He wanted his friends to visit him to have fun, not to get money. Every morning the man made cookies, hoping to have visitors. He sat on the front porch in the afternoon, waiting to hear the sounds of the children's voices.

Several days later, the man was rocking in his chair, when he heard the children! He was thrilled. When the children came to the porch, they had cards and gifts to give him. He told them he had thrown the money plant away. They said it didn't matter and apologized for not coming to visit. The man smiled, went inside, and brought out a batch of fresh chocolate chip cookies.

The Money Plant

After reading "The Money Plant," answer the following questions.

1. What did the man enjoy most about his day?
   - **A.** baking cookies
   - **B.** visiting with the children
   - **C.** watering his plants
   - **D.** rocking on the front porch

2. What does it mean to nurse a plant back to health?
   - **A.** give the plant medicine
   - **B.** take the plant to a hospital
   - **C.** help the plant grow
   - **D.** cut the plant into pieces

3. The word *crept* in the third paragraph means
   - **A.** to sneak into.
   - **B.** to crawl under.
   - **C.** to run around.
   - **D.** to stop and look.

4. Why did the man decide to give the children the money from the plant?

   ____

   ____

5. Why did the man throw the plant away?

   ____

   ____

   ____

Entry Words

using a dictionary

A **dictionary** gives definitions for words. To make it easier to find a particular word, they are listed in alphabetical order.

This section of the dictionary is missing its entry words. Use the sentences at the bottom to find the definition that makes sense for each bold word. Write each bold word in front of its definition. When you are finished, the entry words should be in alphabetical order.

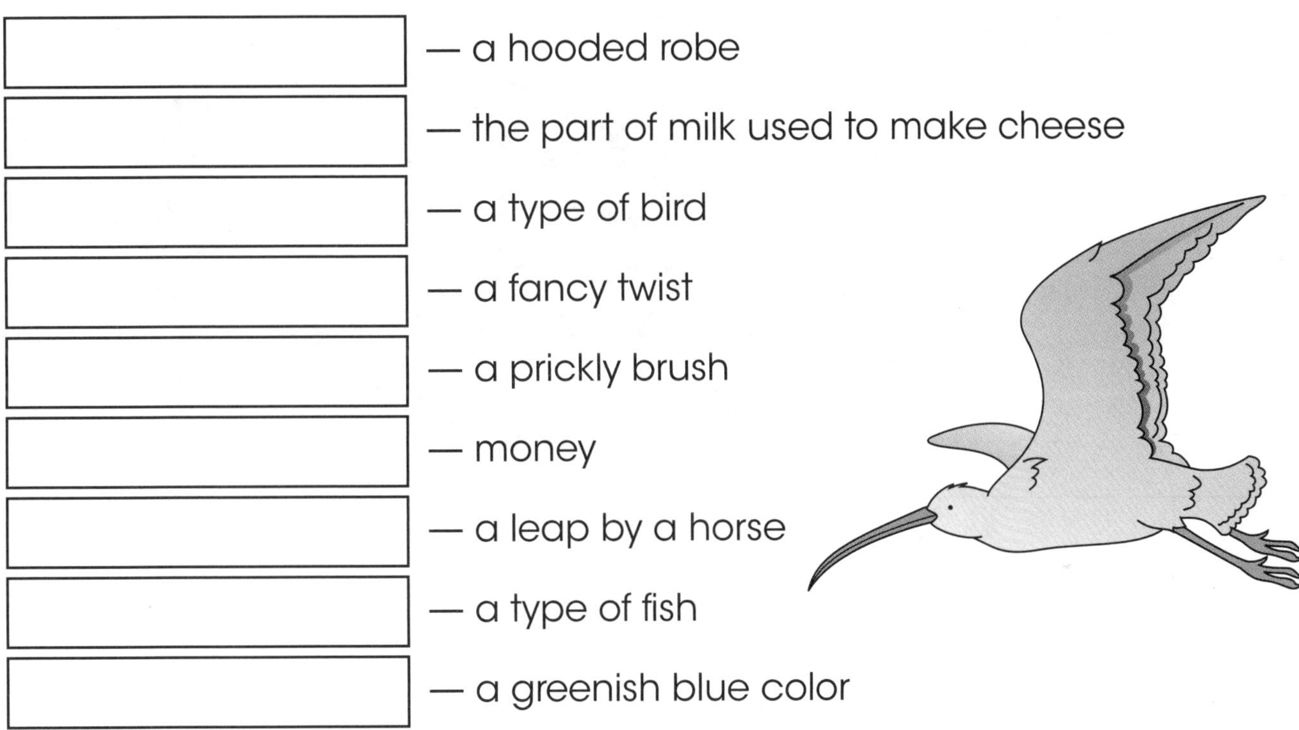

- — a hooded robe
- — the part of milk used to make cheese
- — a type of bird
- — a fancy twist
- — a prickly brush
- — money
- — a leap by a horse
- — a type of fish
- — a greenish blue color

1. The pig had a cute **curlicue** tail.
2. The mysterious traveler wore a **cowl**.
3. My leg is scraped from rubbing against the **currant**.
4. The farmer collected **curd** from the milk pail.
5. In Mexico, the people pay for things with a different **currency**.
6. The ocean looks **cyan** in some places.
7. The **curlew** flew right over our heads!
8. Mom fried **cusk** for dinner.
9. Did you see that horse **curvet**?

Using Guide Words

Guide words are printed in the top corner of each dictionary page. The word on the left is the first entry word on that page. The word on the right is the last entry word on that page. Guide words help "guide" you to the word you need. Flip through dictionary pages looking at guide words to find the page where the words fit.

These entry words are scrambled. Write each word under the correct guide word. Be sure to put the words in alphabetical order.

lamp	locket
low	lobster
loud	learn
large	listen
lane	lot
lion	love

lamb–least

1. **2.**

3. **4.**

licorice–loose

5. **6.**

7. **8.**

lost–lucky

9. **10.**

11. **12.**

Finding Words

A word you look up in a dictionary is called an **entry word**. Its meaning is called a **definition**. If a word has more than one meaning, the definitions are numbered.

Use the dictionary entries below to find the answers.

1. Which definition best fits the word *cry* as it is used in this sentence?

   The little girl cried out for her mother.

   Definition number _____

2. List other forms of the word *cute*. ___________ ___________

3. Which part of speech is the word *cream*? ___________

4. Which definition best fits the word *crook* as it is used in this sentence?

   The crook stole the diamond from the museum.

   Definition number _____

5. What is the definition of the word *dark*?

   ____

cream (noun)
  1. the yellowish white part of milk

crook (noun)
  1. a bent part; curve
I carry my umbrella in the crook of my arm.
  2. a shepherd's staff with a hook at the top
  3. a person who is not honest

cry (verb)
  1. to shed tears; weep.
The hungry baby cried.
  2. to call out loudly; shout.
The people in the burning building were crying for help.

cute (adjective)
  1. delightful or pretty.
This is the cutest puppy I have ever seen.

dark (adjective)
  1. having little or no light
The night was dark because the clouds covered the moon.

dash (verb)
  1. to move fast; rush
We dashed to the waiting bus.
  2. to destroy or ruin
Spraining my ankle dashed my hopes of running in the race.

Mistaken Identity

using a dictionary

1. Once, a rabbi was traveling with his devoted students. It had been a long day. They decided to stop for the night. They found an inn where they could sleep.

2. This inn was a popular stopping place for travelers. It was quite crowded. However, the innkeeper wanted to please the rabbi. So, he gave the rabbi and his students one of his best rooms, the one at the back on the inn.

3. The room was quiet and very dark because there were no windows. The rabbi slept on the only bed. His students scattered mats on the floor around him.

4. It was a misfortune in the end. But, who was to know it would happen? One student had to take an early train back to the city, so he slept close to the door. It would be easier to hear the morning call to wake.

5. The innkeeper rapped softly at the door in the early morning hours. The student did not want to disturb his fellows, so he felt around for his clothes in the darkness.

6. By mistake, he put on the rabbi's long, black coat. Hurrying down the cold, lonely streets, he had but one worry—that he might miss his train. He wrapped the coat tightly around him against the cold and took no notice of what he wore.

7. As he entered the train station, the student stood amazed. Turning from side to side in front of a lobby mirror, he became angry. He turned away from the smirks of those who watched him examining himself in the mirror.

8. "What is this?" he exclaimed. Trying to hide his dismay, he faced the mirror again. "That fool of an innkeeper! I asked that he wake me, and instead he woke the rabbi. Now, I have slept in and shall be late for my train!"

Mistaken Identity

1. In the fourth paragraph, "it was a misfortune" probably means that ______
   - **A.** it is not safe to sleep on the floor.
   - **B.** the dark room was the cause of the mistake.
   - **C.** the fortune teller was wrong.

Cause is why something happens. **Effect** is the event that happens. Circle the correct cause of each effect.

2. The rabbi and his students took a room at the back because
   - **A.** they were not important.
   - **B.** the innkeeper was not nice to them.
   - **C.** the inn keeper wanted to please the rabbi.

3. The student put on the rabbi's robe because
   - **A.** it was handy.
   - **B.** he wanted to be a rabbi.
   - **C.** it was dark and he couldn't see.

4. The student thinks he is the rabbi because
   - **A.** he is dreaming.
   - **B.** he is dressed like him.
   - **C.** the mirror is magic.

Homophones are words that sound the same but have different meanings and spellings. Read each word. Look for its homophone in the paragraph shown in ( ). Write the homophone in the blank.

5. awl (1) ________
6. in (1) ________
7. four (2) ________
8. know (3) ________
9. won (4) ________
10. wrapped (5) ________
11. sighed (7) ________
12. bee (8) ________
13. wood (4) ________

A **main verb** is the most important verb in a sentence. It shows action. A **helping verb** joins together with the main verb. Forms of *be* and *have* are helping verbs. Circle each helping verb. Underline each main verb.

14. Once, a rabbi was traveling.
15. His students had scattered their mats on the floor.
16. The student was hurrying.
17. I have slept late this morning!

Animals

parts of a book

Most chapter books and longer informational books have table of contents pages after the title pages. A table of contents page helps the reader find parts of a book more quickly.

Your teacher asks you to write a report about animals. In the report, you must answer all of the questions listed below. It would take a very long time to read the entire book, so you decide to use the table of contents to help you. Write the chapter and page number where you would look to answer each question.

Table of Contents

	Chapter	Page
1. How long do lions live?		
2. How fast do sailfish swim?		
3. What do snakes eat?		
4. How long does it take for robin eggs to hatch?		
5. Do spiders bite?		
6. Where do poison dart frogs live?		
7. What do beavers eat?		
8. How long do turtles live?		

The Library

Read the story below.

Jen was new in town. Her family had just moved from the country. Jen's new house was on the same street as the public library. Jen had never been to a public library. She had only been to the small library at her old school. But, this library was a large, three-story building. From the outside, Jen thought it looked a bit scary.

However, Jen loved books so much that she summoned the courage to go inside the large building. As she walked in the door, Jen stopped. She looked all around. She had never seen so many books in one place. Jen felt overwhelmed. Marie, one of the librarians, noticed Jen standing by the front door. She offered to show Jen around the library. Marie took Jen up the elevator to the third floor, where the children's library was. Marie showed Jen how the books were shelved and how to locate her favorite authors. Then, Marie showed Jen the computers that were used to locate books. At Jen's old school library, she used a card catalog to locate books. The computer made it much simpler. Jen spent hours looking through the books. Finally, Jen chose a mystery book to check out.

Jen took the book with her to the first floor. She walked to the checkout counter. Marie greeted her with a smile. She helped Jen fill out an application for a library card. Then, she helped Jen check out her book. As Jen walked out of the library with her book, she knew she had found a new favorite place.

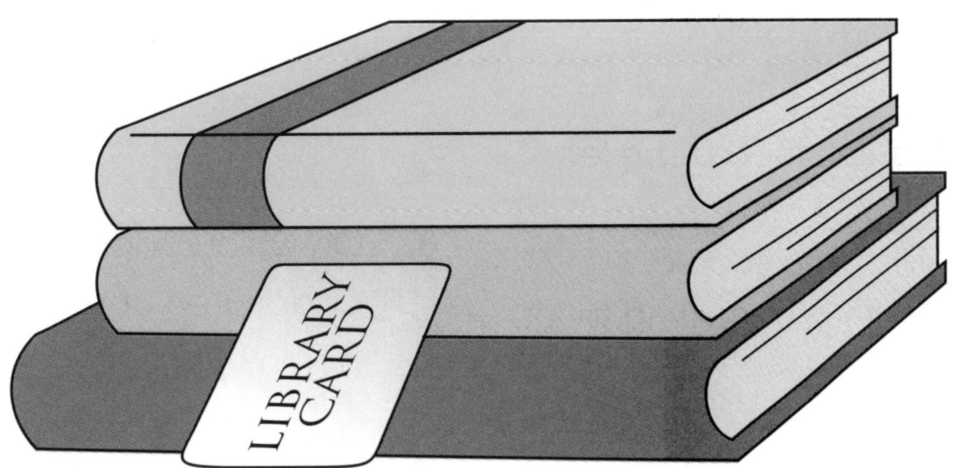

The Library

1. What would be another good title for this story?
   - A. The New Girl
   - B. Jen's First Visit to the Library
   - C. The Nice Librarians

2. Why did Jen think the library looked a bit scary?
   - A. The library was dirty and run-down.
   - B. The library was far away from her house.
   - C. The library was a large, three-story building.

3. What does the word *frozen* mean in this sentence?

   Marie noticed Jen standing frozen.
   - A. not moving
   - B. cold
   - C. icy

4. How did Jen feel as she left the library?
   - A. still a little scared
   - B. tired from reading all of the books
   - C. happy

A **table of contents** is located at the front of a book. It shows what chapters are in the book and on what page each chapter begins. Use the table of contents in the book pictured to answer the questions.

5. Which chapter would tell you if the library is open on October 31?

   ____

6. Which chapter might tell you how to replace a lost library card? ______________

7. Which chapter would tell you the library's street address?

   ____

8. On which page does the chapter on computers begin? ______________

What's In Here?

An **index** is found in the back of many informational books. It contains the main subjects covered in the book and their page numbers. An index lists the main headings for each subject area in alphabetical order. Under each main heading, more specific details might be listed in alphabetical order.

Index

Horses	55, 57–59
Houses	
Cave	34, 41–50
Modern	14, 18, 21
American Indians	67
Humans	
Adults	115–121, 127
Babies	89, 94–108
Children	109–114
Hunting	51, 56
Hurricanes	12, 17

Use the index to find and circle the correct answers.

1. Which page will not help you learn about babies?
   A. page 89 **B.** page 92 **C.** page 97

2. Which page will help you learn about hunting?
   A. page 12 **B.** page 56 **C.** page 115

3. Which type of house is not found in the book?
   A. cave **B.** modern **C.** shingle

4. Which page will not help you learn about houses?
   A. page 76 **B.** page 45 **C.** page 18

5. What will you learn about on page 111?
   A. adults **B.** children **C.** babies

Betsy Ross

Read the passage below.

Betsy Ross was an American hero. She did not fight in wars. She did not become president. She was simply a seamstress. But, her contribution is still remembered today. Betsy Ross made the first United States flag.

In her journal, Betsy Ross wrote about meeting with George Washington in May of 1776. Betsy attended the same church as George Washington. He was a general at the time, and asked Betsy to create a flag for the new country that would soon earn its independence. In July of 1776, the Declaration of Independence declared that the United States was independent from Britain. On June 14, 1777, Congress decided that the flag Betsy Ross made would be the flag of the United States. The flag was to represent the unity of the 13 colonies as one country. The new flag was first flown over Fort Stanwix, New York, on August 3, 1777.

Today, the U.S. flag has 50 stars, representing the country's 50 states. The 13 stripes represent the 13 original colonies. Americans continue to honor the flag and the freedom it represents by saying the Pledge of Allegiance and singing "The Star-Spangled Banner." The U.S. government set aside June 14th as Flag Day to honor the flag.

Betsy Ross

1. What is Betsy Ross best remembered for?
   - **A.** fighting in a war
   - **B.** marrying the president
   - **C.** making the first flag
2. How did Betsy Ross know George Washington?
   - **A.** George Washington was the president.
   - **B.** He was her brother.
   - **C.** They went to the same church.
3. Circle the letter of the sentence that is true.
   - **A.** The stars on the flag represent the 50 states, and the stripes represent the 13 colonies.
   - **B.** The stars on the flag represent the 50 states, and the stripes represent the number of battles won to gain independence.
   - **C.** The stars on the flag represent the 50 heroes of the war, and the stripes represent the 13 colonies.
4. The prefix *uni-* means "one." Write two other words that have the prefix *uni-*.

   ____

   ____

Write each syllable of the words below in the blanks. Use a dictionary to help.

5. contribution ____ ____ ____ ____
6. attended ____ ____ ____
7. representing ____ ____ ____ ____
8. allegiance ____ ____ ____ ____

Read the index below. Then, answer the questions.

9. On what pages could you find the names of the 13 colonies? ____________________
10. What pages might have information about the life of Paul Revere? ____________________
11. On what pages could you find information on Independence Day?

    ____

Look It Up

using an encyclopedia

An **encyclopedia** is a book or set of books containing factual information. On the outside of each book is a letter or letters that show what topics can be found inside that book. Within an encyclopedia, everything is alphabetized. People are alphabetized by their last names.

Write the volume number or numbers that would help you find each answer.

1. Who was the eleventh president of the United States? ______________
2. Who was Babe Ruth? ______________
3. What is the capital of Argentina? ______________
4. Where is the Red Sea located? ______________
5. Where do brown bears live? ______________
6. What does an anaconda eat? ______________
7. What countries were involved in World War I? ______________
8. Who invented the television? ______________

Driver Ants

Read the encyclopedia article. Then, answer the questions on page 90.

Ants can be found almost anywhere on earth. Over 8,000 kinds of ants have been discovered. Ants look the same today as they did when dinosaurs were alive. Scientists found some ants from that time preserved in amber. Amber is tree sap, a sticky liquid. It hardened with the ants stuck inside. The old ants look just like ants do now.

Most ants live in colonies. A colony has one very large queen, and she lays all of the eggs. Most ants are females, but most don't lay eggs. Every ant in a colony has a special job.

The most fearsome ant of all lives in Africa. It is called the driver ant. There can be over 20 million driver ants in one colony.

In a driver ant colony, there are soldier ants that have large mandibles, like very sharp teeth. Their job is to protect the queen and the workers. But, soldier ants can't feed themselves because of their mandibles. It is the job of smaller worker ants to get food and to feed the queen and the soldier ants.

Driver ants are carnivorous, which means that they eat meat. They will eat anything that cannot get away. Sometimes, they eat large animals like cows. However, driver ants mostly eat frogs, spiders, and insects like cockroaches and praying mantises. Driver ant colonies can capture more than 100,000 other insects per day.

People who live in the jungle move out of their huts and villages when they hear that driver ants are coming. After the ants are gone, villagers come back to a home that is free of insects.

Driver ants are nomads. They eat and then move on to find more food. Colonies travel from place to place and do not make permanent homes. If a queen is laying eggs, her colony stops for a short time. They make a nest out of their own bodies. Some ants form walls, and others form the ceiling. When the babies, which are called grubs, can travel, the colony moves on.

Nothing stops driver ants on the move. A colony works well as a team. The ants can build a bridge by climbing and holding onto each other until they reach the other side of a stream. Driver ant colonies have been known to form balls and float on water. What great cooperation!

Driver Ants

1. The main idea of this article is
   - **A.** driver ants like to eat cows.
   - **B.** ants can be found all over the world.
   - **C.** driver ants are remarkable ants.

Details tell more about a main idea. Write the correct details in the blanks.

2. The most fearsome ant is the ______________________.

3. Driver ants usually eat ________, __________, and __________.

Cause is why something happens. **Effect** is the thing that happens. Circle the correct cause of each cause.

4. When driver ants are coming
   - **A.** they hum as they go.
   - **B.** people move out of their way.
   - **C.** the queen lays eggs.

Write *C* if a sentence is complete. Write *I* if a sentence is incomplete.

____ **5.** Over 8,000 different kinds.

____ **6.** Ants are found almost everywhere on earth.

____ **7.** With the ants stuck inside.

____ **8.** After the ants are.

____ **9.** Driver ants are nomads.

____ **10.** The colony works very well as a team.

Topics in an encyclopedia are in alphabetical order. Write the number of the volume listed below in which you would find each topic.

11. dinosaur ____________________

12. ant ____________________

13. jungle ____________________

14. insect ____________________

15. Africa ____________________

Assignments

Charts and **tables** are helpful in organizing information. To read a chart, match your given information from the top and side labels to find new information in the boxes.

Example: What assignment is due in math class on Tuesday?

Find the subject, math, along the top and follow it down to Tuesday's row. You will find *p. 23–24* in the box.

	Reading	Writing	Math	Science	S. Studies
Monday	unit 1	brainstorm	p. 21–22	plant seeds	none
Tuesday	unit 2	rough draft	p. 23–24	none	finish map
Wednesday	unit 3	edit	p. 25–26	record growth	none
Thursday	unit 4	revision	p. 27–28	none	time line
Friday	review	final draft	line graph	record growth	none

Use the information from the chart to find the answers.

1. What assignment is due on Wednesday in Science? ______________
2. What assignment is due on Thursday in Writing? ______________
3. On what day is the time line due in Social Studies? ______________
4. In what subject is the assignment to complete pages 27–28 for Thursday? ______________
5. What assignment is due on Monday in Social Studies? ______________
6. On what day is unit 2 due in Reading? ______________
7. On what day is the line graph due in Math? ______________
8. What assignment is due Tuesday in Writing? ______________

Television Schedule

Use the television schedule below to answer the questions on page 93.

	7:30	8:00	8:30	9:00	9:30	10:00	10:30
2	Jump Start	Make a Million Game Show		The Wild, Wild West		News	
4	Your Lucky Guess	You Should Know!	Wednesday Night at the Movies *Friends Forever*			News	
5	Best Friends	Mary's Secret	Where They Are	Time to Hope	The Tom Show	News	
7	123 Oak Street	Lost Alone	Once Again	Sports Baseball		News	
9	Your Health	Eating Right	Food News	Cooking With Kate		Home Decorating	
11	Silly Rabbit	Bill the Clown	Lots o' Fun	Slime & Rhyme	The Cartoon Connection		Shop Now
24	Trading Your House		Sibling Swap	Sing a Song	Star Lights	Fun & Games	Stuper Star
36	New York Detectives		Rex the Racoon and Mia the Mouse		Special Movie Presentation *Super Kids*		

Television Schedule

1. What does the schedule on page 92 show?
   - **A.** times and channels of television shows
   - **B.** times and channels of radio programs
   - **C.** the number of people that like different shows

2. On what channels can you watch news at 10:00?
   - **A.** 2, 5, and 11
   - **B.** 3, 4, and 11
   - **C.** 2, 4, 5, and 7

3. What time is the show *Silly Rabbit*?
   - **A.** 7:00
   - **B.** 7:30
   - **C.** 8:30

4. What is the Wednesday night movie?
   - **A.** *Lost Alone*
   - **B.** *Mary's Secret*
   - **C.** *Friends Forever*

Circle the word that does not belong in each group.

5. food cook smile eat

6. slime rhyme clown time

7. talk whisper laugh shout

8. funny serious humorous silly

Correctly add the suffix *-ing* to the following words.

9. shop ____________________

10. decorate ____________________

11. eat ____________________

12. laugh ____________________

13. cook ____________________

14. Number the shows in alphabetical order.

____ Make a Million

____ Lucky Guess

____ Mary's Secret

____ Make Me Laugh

Answer Key

Page 9

1. attach; 2. loud; 3. cash; 4. joy; 5. scatter; 6. under; 7. smell; 8. talk; 9. mad; 10. sparkle; 11. odd; The second car should be circled.

Page 10

Down 1. doctor; 2. smart; 3. crowd; 4. grabbed; 5. bite; Across 6. remember; 7. starving; 8. great

Page 12

1. C.; 2. talk/chatter; 3. walk/stroll; 4. run/dash; 5. jump/leap; 6. laugh/giggle; 7. sleep/snooze; 8. whisper; 9. march; 10. dash; 11. laugh; 12. slumber; 13. chuckled; 14. The part of speech.; 15.–16. Answers will vary.

Page 13

expensive/cheap; part/whole; noisy/silent; clean/filthy; toss/catch; safe/dangerous; end/begin; shrink/stretch; child/adult; scared/brave; forget/remember; serious/playful; A Postage Stamp!

Page 14

1. E.; 2. F.; 3. B.; 4. G.; 5. A.; 6. C.; 7. D.

Page 16

1. F; 2. F; 3. T; 4. T; 5. She says and does the opposite of what they say or do.; 6. south; 7. adorable; 8. white; 9. back; 10. wet; 11. full; 12. began; 13. thought; 14. said; 15. rode; 16. sat

Page 17

1. break; 2. book; 3. mean; 4. tire; 5. land; 6. free; 7. glasses; 8. straw

Page 18

Answers will vary.

Page 20

1. A.; 2. F, T, T, T; 3. piglet/baby pig; sow/mother pig; litter/a group of baby pigs from one mother; nuzzled/cuddled; raised/to help grow up; 4. B.; 5. C.; 6. 2; 7. 1; 8. 1; 9. 2; 10. 2; 11. 1

Page 22

1. What Is the Dead Sea?; 2. The Salty Waters of the Dead Sea; 3. The Uses of the Dead Sea; 4. The Water Cycle of the Dead Sea

Page 23

1. C.; 2. C.; 3. B.

Page 24

1. in trees, underground, under bridges, in cacti; 2. to raise their babies; 3. tree trunks; 4. swallows; 5. desert owl; Extra: Answers will vary.

Page 25

1. in albums; 2. because they like to look at them; 3. old, pretty, stamps from far away places; 4. stamps that were printed incorrectly; Extra: Answers will vary.; No, because a stamp must be from a government post office to mail a letter.

Page 26

1. Topic Sentence: Some people like the fire department at the end of our street, and some people do not.; Supporting Details: My mom and dad think it is great because help could reach us within minutes. Nan's parents do not like it because of all the noise the sirens make.; 2. Topic Sentence: Every evening, Gabriel and his dad look forward to feeding the deer in the backyard.; Supporting Details: Gabriel carries the dried corn from the garage to the edge of the woods. He and his dad spread the corn, then hide behind the edge of the house to watch.; 3. Topic Sentence: Allie worked hard to finish all of her projects at summer camp.; Supporting Details: She tie-dyed her shirt in shades of blue and purple. She glued eyes onto her lion's mask.

Page 28

1. A.; 2. feathers; 3. teeth; 4. eggs; 5. nests; 6. 3, 2, 1, 4; 7. F, T, T, F, F; 8. B.; 9. fly; 10. eat; 11. build; 12. hatch; 13. bring

Page 29

1. B.; 2. A.; 3. C.; 4. B.; 5. A.; 6. B.; 7. C.; 8. C.

Page 30

Down 1. sunflower; 4. blooms; 5. stalk; Across 1. sun; 2. center; 3. petals; 4. bud; 6. taproot

Page 32

1. My; 2. her; 3. his; 4. their; 5. your; 6. B.; 7. B.; 8. B.; 9. A.; 10. C.

Answer Key

Page 33

1. different; 2. different; 3. same; 4. same; 5. same; 6. different; 7. different; 8. different; Extra: Answers will vary.

Page 34

Answers will vary.

Page 36

1. B.; 2. F, T, T, F; 3. ostrich: have feather, lays eggs, grows to be 8 feet tall, protective of young; other birds: can fly, have feathers, lays eggs, protective of young; 4. eight; 5. two; 6. weigh; 7. male; 8. r; 9. est; 10. st; 11. est

Page 37

1. Babylonians; 2. the United States and Europe; 3. to stay healthy

Page 38

1. Birds of Prey; 2. after; 3. Wildcat Wackiness, Penguins on Parade; 4. The Reptile Review; 5. The Monkey Movie; 6. Penguin Palace

Page 39

1. 1, 2, before, now; 2. 2, 1, soon, immediately; 3. 1, 2, first, next; 4. 1, 2, earlier, finally; 5. 1, 2, right away, eventually; 6. 2, 1, someday, soon; 7. 1, 2, eventually, never; 8. 2, 1, this week, today

Page 40

4, 2, 3, 6, 1, 5

Page 41

Page 43

1. to avoid getting hurt; 2. C.; 3. tires, brakes, handlebars, pedals; 4. reflectors, helmet, bright colored clothing, laced shoes; 5. A

Page 44

1789–1799: Adams, Washington; 1800–1849: Van Buren, Polk, Monroe, Jefferson; 1850–1899: Cleveland, Grant, Lincoln; 1900–1949: Roosevelt, Wilson, Truman, Hoover; 1950–1999: Clinton, Ford, Kennedy, Reagan; 2000–2007: G. W. Bush

Page 45

1. sock; 2. Uranus; 3. orange; 4. apple; 5. dolphin; 6. pink; 7. mirror; 8. heart; 9. arm; 10. pit; 11. window; 12. baseball; Extra: Answers will vary.

Page 47

1. A; 2. A; 3. land/sea; ground/sky; wild/tame; few/many; small/tall; 4. animals, ants, giraffes, mammals, insects, reptiles, amphibians, cows, birds, trees; 5. whale; 6. giraffe; 7. dog; 8. snake; 9. rabbit

Page 48

1. polite, friendly; 2. stubborn, selfish; 3. sorry, nice

Page 50

1. B.; 2. C.; 3. A.; 4. B.; 5. Answers will vary.

Page 51

1. B.; 2. C.; 3. D.; 4. A.

Page 53

1. 1, 6, 2, 3, 4, 5; 2. B.; 3. C.; 4. C.; 5. take/took; 6. become/became; 7. bring/brought; 8. begin/began; 9. go/went; 10. C; 11. A.; 12. Our cat smelled gas and tried to wake us.; 13. Mom takes in stray animals and she gives them baths.

Page 55

1. C.; 2. B.; 3. A.; 4. preheat; 5. soft peak; 6. cream of tartar; 7. teaspoon; 8. drizzle

Page 56

1. Dancing is a valued tradition among several American Indian tribes.; 2. They dance for birthdays and marriage ceremonies.; 3. By dancing in a circle, tribes are able to stay symbolically connected to their family and traditions.; 4. Their dances are very exciting.; 5. The dances are beautiful and graceful.; 6. American Indian Dances are the best in the world.

Page 58

1. C.; 2. Answers will vary.; 3. to gulp air to help them stay upright; 4. A.; 5. Answers will vary.

Answer Key

Page 60

1. F; 2. O; 3. F; 4. O; 5. A.; 6. B.; 7. The king of France and two brothers; 8. A major in the army and a physics professor; 9. Ed Yost and Raven Industries; 10. Ed Yost and the Navy; 11. think; 12. do; 13. begin; 14. sell

Page 61

1. A.; 2. B., C.; 3. B., C., D.

Page 62

1. no; 2. yes; 3. yes; 4. no; 5. yes; 6. no; 7. no

Page 63

(Mammals) Alike: thumb and fingers, drink milk, born alive, similar ears and nose; Different: wings; (Birds) Alike: wings; Different: feathers; Mammal; Answers will vary.

Page 65

1. The first prince on the left; 2. T, T, F, F, T; 3. gentle/men; 4. horse/shoe; 5. hand/book; 6. god/mother; 7. wrist/watch; 8. Answers will vary.; 9. verb: has, subject: shirt, object: buttons; 10. verb: is wearing, subject: prince, object:crown; 11. verb: read, subject: Cinderella, object: book; 12. ugly; 13. happy, content; 14. lose; 15. forget

Page 67

1. B.; 2. C.; 3.–7. Answers will vary. 8. warm, warmest; 9. happy, happiest; 10. short, shortest; 11. old, oldest; 12. high, highest; 13. because it was too warm in spring and the snow would melt; 14. showers, sun warming the

Page 67 continued

earth; 15. shorter days, longer nights, crisp, cool air

Page 68

1. B.; 2. A.; 3. C.

Page 69

Answers will vary.

Page 71

1. A. Put a sock in it., B. jumped out of their skins, C. dead to the world; 2. little; 3. skin; 4. antsy; 5. lollygag; 6.–7. Answers will vary.

Page 72

Answers will vary.

Page 73

Answers will vary.

Page 76

1. B.; 2. C.; 3. A.; 4. because they nursed the plant back to health; 5. because he thought the kids only wanted to visit him to get money

Page 77

cowl, curd, curlew, curlicue, currant, currency, curvet, cusk, cyan

Page 78

1. lamp; 2. lane; 3. large; 4. learn; 5. lion; 6. listen; 7. lobster; 8. locket; 9. lot; 10. loud; 11. love; 12. low

Page 79

1. 2; 2. cuter, cutest; 3. noun; 4. 3; 5. having little or no light

Page 81

1. B.; 2. C.; 3. C.; 4. B.; 5. all; 6. inn; 7. for; 8. no; 9. one; 10. rapped; 11. side; 12. be;

Page 81 continued

13. would; 14. helping verb: was, main verb: traveling; 15. helping verb: had, main verb: scattered: 16. helping verb: was, main verb: hurrying; 17. helping verb: have, main verb: slept

Page 82

1. 3, 3; 2. 4, 35; 3. 2, 13; 4. 6, 57; 5. 5, 49; 6. 3, 21; 7. 3, 3; 8. 2, 13

Page 84

1. B.; 2. C.; 3. A.; 4. C.; 5. 15; 6. 9; 7. 5; 8. 11

Page 85

1. B.; 2. B.; 3. C.; 4. A.; 5. B.

Page 87

1. C.; 2. C.; 3. A.; 4. unify, unicycle; 5. con/tri/bu/tion; 6. at/tend/ed; 7. rep/re/sent/ing; 8. al/le/giance; 9. 5, 7-9, 22; 10. 6, 28-30; 11. 19, 25;

Page 88

1. 10, 14; 2. 11; 3. 1; 4. 11; 5. 2; 6. 1; 7. 15; 8. 13

Page 90

1. C.; 2. driver ant; 3. frogs, spiders, insects; 4. B.; 5. I; 6. C.; 7. I; 8. I; 9. C.; 10. C.; 11. 3; 12. 1; 13. 6; 14. 5; 15. 1

Page 91

1. record growth; 2. revision; 3. Thursday; 4. Math; 5. none; 6. Tuesday; 7. Friday; 8. rough draft

Page 93

1. A.; 2. C.; 3. B.; 4. C.; 5. smile; 6. clown; 7. laugh; 8. serious; 9. shopping; 10. decorating; 11. eating; 12. laughing; 13. cooking; 14. 2, 1, 4, 3